MACBETH
A RESOURCE TEXT FOR STUDENTS

Wendy Lynch

BASIL BLACKWELL

First published 1988

Published by
Basil Blackwell Limited
108 Cowley Road
Oxford OX4 1JF

Shakespeare, William, *1564–1616*
   Macbeth: a resource text for students.
   I. Title   II. Lynch, Wendy
   822.3'3

   ISBN 0-631-90138-8

Acknowledgements

The author and publisher would like to thank the following for
permission to reproduce illustrative material: (v, 3 left, 4) The
Folger Shakespeare Library: (3 right) Geographers' A–Z map com-
pany Ltd and HMSO; (8) The International Shakespeare Globe
Centre Ltd; (13) Private Eye; (135 above left, 136 above right)
Zoe Dominic; (136 above left) BBC Enterprises Ltd; (135 below
left and above right, 136 below left) The National Film Archive
London.

The review 'Macbeth at Stratford' by Kenneth Tynan (p 137) is
reprinted from 'A view of the English stage' by permission of
Methuen London.

The extract on p 139 is from 'The Macbeth Murder Mystery' in
Vintage Thurber vol I, copyright 1963 by James Thurber, by
permission of Hamish Hamilton Ltd.

Line drawings by Leslie Marshall are based on original ideas by
Roger Vasey.

Set in 10 on 11 pt Horley Old Style and 9 on 11 Helvetica Light
by Multiplex techniques ltd, St Mary Cray, Kent

Printed by Butler & Tanner Ltd, Frome, Somerset

Contents

Old City of London – with Globe, Thames.

A Day in the Life of William Shakespeare

Although we do not have a great many details about William Shakespeare's life, there is enough information to put together a likely picture of his lifestyle. Here is an imaginary reconstruction of a typical day in his life in the year 1606.

I lodge in the house of Christopher Mountjoy, the wig-maker in Silver Street, and my awakenings are never gentle. His family must be the noisiest in Cripplegate! Getting dressed is no problem because I own so few garments. Doublet, hose and tunic for everyday and a more elaborate set and ruff for special occasions. I'd rather invest my money than wear it. I break my fast simply with rye bread and ale. I never thought I'd find a new vice at my age but I have to admit that I take pleasure in the new tobacco smoking habit.

Audiences are getting harder and harder to please. We now have to perform fifteen different plays in a month. My life sometimes seems one long rehearsal. And when we're not rehearsing, we're performing – every afternoon while it's light – except on Sunday.

Things at the theatre have been looking up since James became King. He's a reader, a writer and he loves acting and plays. Our audiences have risen sharply since he became our sponsor and we became the King's Men. Nothing like a command performance for swelling the coffers! I have just completed *Macbeth* which the King says is his favourite play. That's not surprising. It wasn't totally by accident that I wrote about his favourite subject – witches – and his noble Scottish ancestor, Banquo!

We perform many of our plays in the Globe Theatre which is south of the river Thames. I can just see it from my bedroom window. We moved there seven years ago after the lease on the old Theatre in Shoreditch had run out and it's so easy for me to reach. Sometimes I take the wherry across the river from the bottom of Bread Street. When I'm feeling energetic I'll cross London Bridge. Most of my work is performed at the Globe, but we've no choice but to do tours in the winter months. I hate all the travelling and the bad weather and the problems.

When the morning rehearsal is over, I tend to have a simple meal of chicken and sack at The Anchor Inn next to the theatre. Recently we've been having problems with the casting for *Macbeth* and breaks are very welcome. With only fifteen of us to cover all the parts, there's often squabbling and fighting. You know what actors are like! Sometimes I may take my lunch in Silver Street. I much prefer living here to my previous lodgings in Bishopsgate and Southwark which were damp and unpleasant. My son Hamnet died of the Spanish fever when he was only eleven and I've always suspected that he must have caught the disease when he and the family came to visit me in London. That's one of the reasons I bought a big house in Stratford called New Place where Anne can bring up the girls in safety.

Performances are at two. The Globe's a fine theatre to perform in – much more space than the old Theatre at Shoreditch and a good atmosphere too. Dick Burbage is our best actor. He breathes life into the Macbeth of my imagination. Even the groundlings are hushed when he's on stage. Robert Armin is our comic actor. When he plays the Porter the air fills with raucous laughter and cheers. One day he accepted drinks from the groundlings and barely finished the scene on his feet! I love acting too but never have enough time for anything but small parts. I'm playing the Doctor in *Macbeth* so I can do a little more writing before I come on stage.

When performances are over *The Anchor* and *The Mermaid* do good business. I'll join the players for the inevitable sack and bragging sessions, but all the time I know I have to get back to my work. I've been re-reading a book by Plutarch about the Romans and already I think I've got some good ideas for a plot.

The time I like best is when my work is over for the day. I might stroll to *The Mermaid* for a tankard or two of ale with Ben Jonson. He writes plays for our company. We're both great talkers and soon the air is full of the failure of the Gunpowder Plot or new ways of acting or who's the best playwright in London. Writers never stop working, of course, and the tavern's a great place for meeting new people and hearing travellers' tales. I don't get to Stratford as often as I'd like and I hate the solitary life.

Sometimes I go straight home and to bed, other times I like to take a longer walk. On a fine, warm summer's evening I make my way towards London Bridge and listen to the raucous roar of the Thames boatmen with their 'Eastward Ho!' and 'Westward Ho!'. The houses and shops which line London Bridge are always throbbing with life. Yet in the midst of all this warmth and bustle, I can never pass the Bridge Gate without a shudder of sympathy at the poor devils whose heads are on the spikes. Life's but a walking shadow.

Activities

1 Look at the old map of the City of London on the next page. Using the information given above, locate the areas of Shakespeare's lodgings and the theatres he worked in. In groups, trace the places Shakespeare might have visited on a typical day and discuss how they might have looked. It may help to do some research on the subject. Dover Wilson's *Life in Shakespeare's England* will give you some further information.

2 Look at the new map of the City of London on the next page. Again working in groups, discuss the differences between the old and the new. (Work is at present taking place to build a new Globe Theatre on its original site.)

3 In groups, using hints from 'A Day in the Life of William Shakespeare', as well as your own imagination, discuss what sort of a man you think Shakespeare might have been.

4 Now, working on your own, imagine that Shakespeare has been granted a wish to return to the City of London in the 20th century and tries to revisit his old lodgings and the theatres he used to know. Describe what he sees and his thoughts and feelings as he does so. Call your account 'London Revisited'.

Important dates in Shakespeare's life

1564 – William Shakespeare was born in Stratford upon Avon.

1568 – Shakespeare's father, John, became Mayor of Stratford.

1582 – Shakespeare, aged 18, married Anne Hathaway.

1583 – First daughter, Susanna, was born.

1585 – Twins, Hamnet and Judith, were born.

1586 – Shakespeare left his wife and family behind and went to London to act and to write plays. He lived in Bishopsgate near both the Theatre and the Curtain in Shoreditch.

1592 – The Plague struck London so the theatres had to close. Shakespeare began to write poetry and the Earl of Southampton became his patron. (See Glossary)

1594 – The Theatre re-opened. Shakespeare joined in the formation of a new acting company called the Lord Chamberlain's Men. (Elizabeth I had decreed that all acting companies should take their names from noble men.) The Lord Chamberlain's Men performed mainly in the Theatre north of the city, but also before the Queen. They also went on winter tours.

1596 – Hamnet, Shakespeare's only son, died aged eleven. Shakespeare moved south of the river to Southwark.

1597 – Shakespeare, now a successful playwright, bought New Place, a large manor house in Stratford.

1599 – The Globe Theatre was built, south of the Thames.

1602 – Shakespeare moved to Silver Street to lodge in the house of Christopher Mountjoy, a wig-maker.

1603 – Queen Elizabeth died. James VI of Scotland became James I of England, uniting the two countries. Shakespeare's acting company was now chosen by James and became known as the King's Men. During this year James published in London two works on witchcraft, *Daemonologie* and *News from Scotland*.

1605 – Gunpowder Plot was discovered.

1606 – *Macbeth* was written.

1608 – The King's Men now occupied a new theatre, Blackfriars, as well as the Globe.

1611 – Shakespeare retired to Stratford.

1613 – The Globe Theatre was destroyed by fire but rebuilt soon after.

1616 – Shakespeare died.

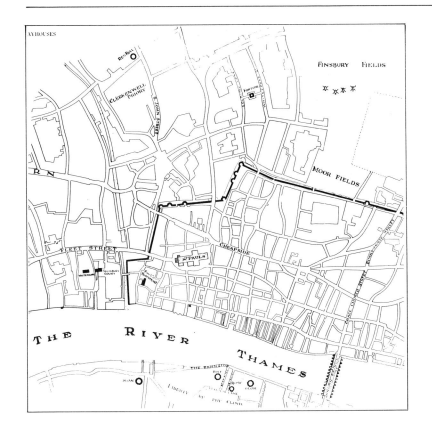

Map of Shakespeare's London

Map of the City of London as it is today.

Based on an Ordnance Survey map. Crown copyright reserved.

Sweaty Nightcaps – An Afternoon at the Globe Theatre

The Globe

Many of Shakespeare's plays were first performed in the Globe Theatre in London. The idea of a special building just for the performance of plays was a relatively new one. The Globe, built in 1599, was one of the earliest theatres in the country. Previously plays had been performed in the inner courtyards of inns. The Globe was a tall structure, roughly circular in shape and constructed out of wood. This is why Shakespeare described its shape in one of his plays as 'this wooden O'.

Spectators could either stand around the stage or if they had money, they could get a better view from a seat in one of the three galleries that ran round the theatre. The galleries and the stage had canopies over them covered with thatch. However, the cheap standing part of the theatre was open to the sky.

Performances took place in the afternoon while it was still light. Women were not allowed to act so all the female roles were taken by boy actors. While the actors' costumes were often very elaborate, less emphasis was placed on scenery and props. For example a wood such as Birnam Wood in *Macbeth*, might be represented by a simple arrangement such as a few branches. Usually there was no scenery at all. Performances tended to be loud, noisy affairs with lots of audience participation. They were, in fact, more like a pantomime or even a football match of today. Shakespeare in another play, *Julius Caesar*, described a large, noisy crowd of people like this.

'The rabblement hooted, and clapp'd their chopt hands and threw up their sweaty night caps.'

He could well have been thinking of a group of spectators in the theatre. All sorts of people visited the theatre from the grandest courtier to the most humble apprentice. In 1599 a Swiss doctor called Thomas Platter described a visit to the London theatres like this: 'Daily at two in the afternoon London has two, sometimes three plays running in different places, competing with each other, and those which are best obtain most spectators'.

Here is an imaginary account of a visit to the Globe Theatre, seen through the eyes of Thomas Pinchinbeck and Benjamin Underberry, two young shoemakers of the time. They are enjoying a holiday.

'Come on then, Tom, it's time to go', said Benjamin, trying to drag his reluctant friend out of the alehouse.

'Not yet, there's plenty of time for another drink', said Tom.

'You promised you'd come to the play and you've had too much ale already.'

'All right then, Ben,' he said, getting up from his seat, 'I'm coming. What is this play you keep talking about, anyway?'

'It's Will Shakespeare's latest. It's called *Macbeth*. They were all talking about it last week. It's got some witches and magical spells and lots of killing.'

'Witches? I don't know if I want to see witches. Is it safe to go?'

'Of course it is. It's only a play', said Ben. 'Come on, hurry, we're almost there. There's the theatre in the distance.'

The two men had by now left the alehouse and reached the narrow street leading to the Globe. That day, being a holiday, the streets were crowded and full of noise. Noblemen and vagabonds, merchants and thieves, pedlars and pickpockets all pushed against each other down the street. Two street musicians played their cornets. 'What is 't you lack gentlemen?' came the cry from the street sellers. Ahead, the flag bearing the sign of the Globe fluttered and furled its way up the flag-pole.

'Quick,' cried Ben, 'the flag's going up. We'll have to hurry, it's about to begin.'

Suddenly the tall shape of the Globe reared up before them and the force of the crowd propelled them towards the narrow doorway.

'How much is it?' asked Tom, fumbling for a coin.

'Just one penny', said the gatherer at the door. 'That's if you're standing in the pit. Twopence for a seat in the gallery and threepence for the upper gallery.'

'Two for the pit', said Ben, and in they both went.

They joined hundreds of other groundlings jostling for position near the stage. Although the stage was large and jutted well out into the pit, Ben wanted to get close to it for he enjoyed the exchanges with the actors.

'Can you see all right there, Tom?'

'No, I can't. There are some people sitting on the stage. They're not actors, are they?'

'Of course they're not. The actors are behind those two doors at the back of the stage, the tiring house, where they put on their robes.'

'Who are the ones on the stage, then?'

'People with more money than we have. They can afford to sit on the stage. Anyway we'll move a bit so you can see.'

'That's better.'

'Ssh now', said Ben, as the trumpet sounded, announcing the start of the play.

The crowd went quiet. There was a tremendous crash of thunder. Up out of a small trap at the front of the stage arose a cauldron. A door at the back of the stage opened and the frightening figure of a witch appeared and moved forward.

'When shall we three meet again,
In thunder, lightning or in rain?' she called.
From the other door, a second witch emerged, saying,
'When the hurlyburly's done,
When the battle's lost and won.'
Then another trap in the stage opened and a third witch cackled,
'That will be ere the set of sun.'

Tom turned to Ben, 'She's ugly. I didn't know your sister was in the play!'

Ben grinned but kept his eyes on the action unfolding before him.

When the witches had finished their scene, shouts and clapping filled the theatre and it was some time before Tom could make himself heard.

'I hope we're not going to get wet. That thunder sounded close.'

'It's not real thunder', said Ben. 'It's part of the play. They make the noise by rolling cannon balls over the wooden floor above the stage.'

The theatre was suddenly filled with cheers and whistles from all around as the crowd spotted Dick Burbage making his way onto the stage. Some of the spectators were drinking ale and others were walking from place to place to greet old friends or get a better view.

'Ssh', said Ben. 'That's Dick Burbage.'

'Who's he then?'

'Don't you know anything? He's the best player. He'll be playing Macbeth. He's the one we've all paid to see.'

The man next to Tom suddenly shouted out,

'Come on Dick, give us a good show.'

Burbage, dressed in armour as Macbeth, smiled and bowed low. Then,

Inside the Globe

as the drums sounded, his expression changed and, taking up his position on the stage he began to speak in a true, clear voice that could be heard equally well by those in the pit and those in the top gallery,

'So foul and fair a day I have not seen.'

The play unfolded through the long afternoon with the crowd uproarious and silent by turns. As the swords flashed in the final battle scene, the crowd roared on their heroes and booed and hissed the villains. The play ended in a tumult of applause and appreciative shouts as the actors returned to the stage to take their bow.

Tom and Ben joined the crowd thronging out through the Globe's narrow door into the crowded street.

'Well, then, your first visit to the theatre. What did you think of it?' asked Ben. 'You certainly shouted enough comments to the actors.'

'I've had a good time', said Tom. 'It was much better than I expected. I really liked the Porter at the gate of Macbeth's castle. I think he'd had more to drink than we had. He even took a drink from the flagon of the man next to me. If that's acting, I think I would like to become an actor, not a shoemaker!'

With all this talk of drink, Tom had already begun to think of a second visit to the alehouse. 'That was a good afternoon', he said. 'When you go to theatre again, I'll come with you. What's on next?'

'Well, they do a different play nearly every day. I am not sure what the next one's called, but it's about a king who gets murdered in Denmark.'

'I like a good murder', said Tom. 'If Burbage is in it, I'll come with you!'

Activities

1 From this account it is clear that a visit to the theatre in Shakespeare's time was very different from a theatre visit today. Make a list of the most important differences.

2 Imagine that a time machine allows Tom and Ben to visit a theatre today to watch a play. Write a conversation that might take place between them during and after the performance. Choose any play you know for them to watch, or use an imaginary one.

3 A new Globe Theatre is at present being built on its original site in Southwark. An artist's impression of this is shown on the next page. Find out all you can about the new Globe and in particular check on the similarities between the original Globe and this one. The 'Shakespeare and Schools' project publishes a termly newsletter that gives up to date information on the new Globe. You may also find further information by writing to

International Shakespeare Globe Centre (ISGC)
Bear Gardens
Bankside
Liberty of the Clink
Southwark
London SE1 9EB

An artist's impression of the new Globe Theatre

The Weird Sisters – Magic and Mystery

Much of the magic and mystery that occurs throughout *Macbeth* surrounds three witches whom Macbeth describes as 'the weird sisters'. *Weird* comes from the Old English 'wyrd' which means *fate*. No one is exactly sure where the word *witch* comes from but it is likely that it was derived from *wit*, the old word for knowledge. Witches were people who had, or were thought to have, forbidden knowledge. This knowledge became known as *witchcraft*. Both men and women were believed to practise witchcraft, but most witchcraft stories and legends tend to be about women.

At the time that Shakespeare wrote *Macbeth* there was enormous interest in witches. This was partly due to the fact that King James I was fascinated by witchcraft and had written several books on the subject. Here are some early descriptions of how witches were supposed to look and the powers they were believed to have.

What witches looked like

'A witch is an old weather-beaten crone, having her chin and her knees meeting for age, walking like a bow leaning on a shaft, hollow-eyed, untoothed, furrowed on her face, having her lips trembling with the palsy, going mumbling in the streets.'

Bishop Bancroft, 1603.

What witches could do

'They can raise storms and tempest in the air either upon sea or land, though not universally, but in such prescribed bounds as God will permit them.'

James I, *Daemonologie* 1603

Witches were also said to possess the power to:
- ride in the air;
- disappear in the air;
- raise winds, hail, thunder and lightning;
- make ships leak (though not sink);
- turn themselves into any animal (but the animal would not have a tail, so you would always know it was a witch).

Witchcraft taught people how to harm those they wished to hurt. Waxen figures of the intended victim were stuck with needles or melted before a slow fire. As the figure melted or wasted, so the intended victim suffered the same fate.

How witches worked

'Witches worketh by the devil, or by some devilish or curious art, either hurting or healing, revealing things secret, or fortelling things to come, which the devil hath devised to entangle and snare men's souls withal to damnation.'

Gifford 1597

Witches were instructed or controlled by *familiars* or *imps* who took the form of animals – usually cats, but also dogs, ravens or toads. It was through these familiars that they were able to see into the future. Below is a picture of a woman accused of witchcraft and brought to trial by the Witch Finder General, Matthew Hopkins. Notice the names she gives to her *imps*.

A witch's confession

In 1604, witchcraft became a capital offence. If there was evidence of a relationship with evil spirits, a suspect was condemned to death by hanging, burning or drowning.

Here is a description by James I of a famous witch trial:
A certain Agnis Tompson, with a coven of Scottish witches from Forres, was put on trial charged with trying to cause the death of James I by shipwreck off the coast of Scotland. In court she confessed 'that she took

Matthew Hopkins, Witch Finder General

a black toad and did hang the same up by the heels, three days, and collected the venom as it dropped and fell from it, – in an oyster shell, and kept the same venom close covered...she took a cat and christened it, and afterwards bound to each part of the cat the chiefest parts of a dead man, and several joints of his body...in the night the cat was conveyed into the midst of the sea by all these witches sailing in their riddles or sieves, and left right before the town of Lieth in Scotland: this done, there did arise such a tempest in the sea, as a greater has not been seen...The said witch declared that his Majesty had never come safely from the sea if his faith had not prevailed above their intentions.'

James I, *News from Scotland, 1603*

A 20th-century view

Although many of Shakespeare's contemporaries would have believed in witches as servants of the devil, some would share the modern view that many so-called witches were really nothing more than women who were mentally disturbed, or who behaved in an eccentric way or who had an odd appearance. Evil people undoubtedly sometimes made use of the popular fear of witches to persecute their enemies. Even today the term *witch hunt* is used by politicians and others who feel that they are being pursued by enemies unjustly.

Activities

1 Make a list of all the powers that witches were believed to have in the 17th century.
2 You have won first prize in a competition which allows you to be a witch or a wizard for a day! Using what you know about witchcraft, describe how you would spend your day.
3 Imagine that you are a reporter for a modern newspaper who, by some strange quirk of time, has managed to attend a witch's trial. Write a newspaper headline and a report of the trial itself, making use of the information in this chapter as well as any other information you can find.

Killing a king – a crime against God

Whenever we study a Shakespeare play, it is especially important to look closely at the major events that were taking place around the time that it was written. This may help us to understand particular issues that occur in the play and may give us a better insight into character and plot. Certainly as far as *Macbeth* is concerned, many of the major themes reflect contemporary events. There is strong emphasis in the play on the need to ensure that the throne is occupied by a rightful king. This is not accidental. Shakespeare was very concerned to please his Royal Patron James I who had just succeeded to the English throne.

James had been made king of England in 1603. Prior to this he had been ruling over Scotland as James VI. He was the first king ever to rule over both England and Scotland together. He had a right to both thrones as the family tree below shows.

Additionally, his own Scottish ancestors were those very people who triumphed in *Macbeth* and brought a legitimate king and peace to strife-torn Scotland. In writing the play, and glorifiying the King's Scottish ancestors, Shakespeare was to some extent expressing the general relief of the nation at the prospect of unity and stability James had brought.

One other theme of the play was the Divine Right of kings. This was the belief, widely felt at the time, that kings got their power from God

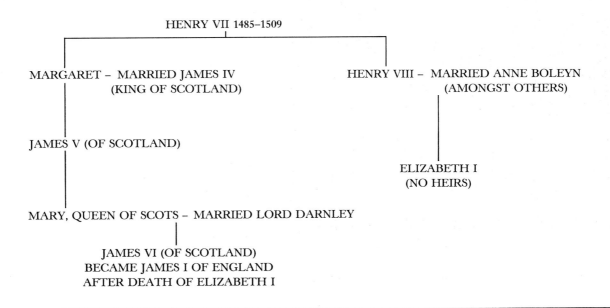

HENRY VII 1485–1509

MARGARET – MARRIED JAMES IV
(KING OF SCOTLAND)

HENRY VIII – MARRIED ANNE BOLEYN
(AMONGST OTHERS)

JAMES V (OF SCOTLAND)

ELIZABETH I
(NO HEIRS)

MARY, QUEEN OF SCOTS – MARRIED LORD DARNLEY

JAMES VI (OF SCOTLAND)
BECAME JAMES I OF ENGLAND
AFTER DEATH OF ELIZABETH I

and that any attack upon the king was an attack upon God himself. In 1605, such an attack was made upon James I in what is generally called the Gunpowder Plot. At the time Shakespeare was writing *Macbeth* the whole of England was still recovering from the shock of an attempted assassination. This was a direct attack upon James I and was seen as an attack against democracy and against God. Such an event might seem very distant and remote from us, yet to the people of that time, it was every bit as terrible as a modern terrorist outrage. Their reaction may well be compared to the shock and horror felt in Britain amongst people of all political parties when the IRA almost succeeded in blowing up the Cabinet in Brighton in 1985. Shakespeare was speaking for the nation in *Macbeth* when he stressed the importance of unity, of honesty and loyalty to the king. Threats to the king are also seen as an outrage against God and against the welfare of the country.

Although there was general relief at the arrival of James I, the country was by no means totally peaceful and united. Rivalry between religious groups remained strong. The Roman Catholic community in particular felt oppressed. They had received a succession of blows from the last three rulers of England. Henry VIII had brought Protestantism to England and both Elizabeth I and the new king James clearly intended to keep England Protestant. The Gunpowder Plot, led by a group of fanatical Catholics, was an indication of the unrest amongst the Roman Catholics in the country. In fact it led to even more oppression, and many devout Catholics were forced to lie to avoid detection. In many cases the lie took a particular form that was known as EQUIVOCATION. This involved using words that were open to several meanings in order to mislead. Equivocation plays an important part in *Macbeth*.

Activities

1 Here is an exercise that will help to recreate for you the tremendous significance of the Gunpowder Plot for Shakespeare and his contemporaries.

It is the evening of November 5th 1605. King James I and the Members of Parliament have just survived an attempt on their lives. You are a 20th-century TV news presenter. News is coming in fast. Using the briefing notes below, work in groups to organise your material. (If you can, try to do some further research). Then, 'present' your news using a newsreader, outsider reporters, interviews with witnesses etc, and, if you can gain an audience, with the King himself.

BRIEFING NOTES (Based on a variety of contemporary sources)

JAMES I

Appearance ugly, fat, big nose, small mouth, soft skin, sandy hair and moustache, bandy legs.

Habits never washes, coarse manners, drinks heavily, prefers the company of men to women.

Education/interests well-educated, widely read. Particularly interested in witchcraft (has written on subject), enjoys plays and the theatre.

Religion strict Protestant upbringing. Wants to keep England Protestant. Firmly believes in the Divine Right of Kings.

Character Cowardly. Constantly in fear of assassination. Rarely shows himself in public. Always wears a well-padded doublet to protect himself against any assassination attempt. Generous with money.

SUSPECTS

Thomas Percy, Robert Catesby, Guy Fawkes, amongst others. All Roman Catholics who want a Roman Catholic government.

DETAILS OF PLOT

House rented next to Houses of Parliament by Percy, Catesby and Fawkes, 1604.
Cellars under House of Lords rented by the same people, 1605.
New session of Parliament due to open November 5th 1605. King James and family due to be there.
November 4th, warning letter received by Lord Mounteagle.
'though there be no appearance of any stir, yet I say they shall receive a terrible blow, the Parliament, yet they shall not see who hurts them.'
Cellars searched.
1½ tons of gunpowder, firewood, coal found in cellar.
Slow burning matches found in possession of Fawkes.
Percy, Catesby and Fawkes arrested.

2 Below is a modern cartoon about the Gunpowder Plot. It is based upon a famous picture of the time. Although there were no newspapers in Shakespeare's time, there were pamphlets. Make up your own cartoon about the Plot for one of these contemporary pamphlets.

MACBETH

Text, notes and activities

Act One

SCENE 1

An open place on a moor. Thunder and lightning.
Enter three Witches

First Witch
　　When shall we three meet again?
　　In thunder, lightning, or in rain?
Second Witch
　　When the hurlyburly's done,
　　When the battle's lost and won.
Third Witch
　　That will be ere the set of sun.　　　　　　　　　　5
First Witch
　　Where the place?
Second Witch　　　　　Upon the heath.
Third Witch
　　There to meet with Macbeth.
First Witch
　　I come Graymalkin!
Second Witch
　　Paddock calls.　　　　　　　　　　　　　　　　10
Third Witch　　　Anon!
All
　　Fair is foul, and foul is fair:
　　Hover through the fog and filthy air.

The Witches *vanish*

This scene takes place on an area of waste moorland. It is thundering and lightning. To begin with the place is deserted. **What will be the effect upon the audience?**

3 *hurlyburly* the chaos and confusion of the storm and the battle cries.
4 *lost and won* **Can a battle be lost and won?** The witches may simply be referring to the end of a battle where one side wins and the other side loses. But it is worth noting that they do often speak in riddles.
5 *ere* before.
8 *Macbeth* The Third Witch mentions Macbeth by name. **How does this affect the audience?**
9 *Graymalkin* a grey cat. This would be a *familiar* of the First Witch. A familiar was an assistant to a witch. (See p 9.) It took on the form of a dog, cat or ape but it had the spirit of a demon.
10 *Paddock* a toad and a familiar of the Second Witch. **How would it call?**
11 *Anon* I'm coming now. **What is likely to have brought this response from the Third Witch?**

POINTS TO CONSIDER

? Enter three witches. Bearing in mind the Elizabethan attitude to witches (see notes on The Weird Sisters, p 9), what atmosphere in the theatre is created by their arrival?

? 12 Things are not always what they appear to be on the outside. This is an important idea repeated through the play and is therefore one of its *themes*. What is Shakespeare suggesting here about the world of the Witches?

ACT ONE SCENE 1 SUGGESTED ACTIVITIES

Production/Group Work

P1 Imagine you are producing this scene on stage

  a) in the 20th century
  b) in 1606

In groups, discuss what props, costumes, make-up, music, sound effects, smells and lighting you might use in the two different productions. You might like to look back at the chapter *Sweaty Nightcaps – an Afternoon at the Globe Theatre* (p 4) to remind yourselves about the theatre in Shakespeare's time.

P2 In groups of three, take on the role of the Witches and read the scene aloud. How will you differentiate between the three voices? As you read, listen to the rhythm of their words. What does it sound like? What noises do the words make?

Text

T1 The last but one line of the scene suggest that things may appear to be one thing on the surface but are really different underneath. What famous English proverb means the same? Find out where your proverb comes from.

Written Work

W1 You have already discussed how you might produce this scene. Now, working alone, write out the scene, leaving a space between each line. Then, using a different colour, write in the producer's notes. Swap these with someone else when you have finished and, in pairs, discuss the way each of you has chosen to produce the scene.

W2 You are a newspaper reporter and have been given a tip-off that something strange is going on at the moor near Forres in Scotland. The Editor is going to give you the front page. Write a headline and a report following your visit and sighting of the Witches.

SCENE 2

A camp near Forres.
Alarum within. Enter **King Duncan, Malcolm, Donalbain, Lennox** *with*
Attendants, *meeting a bleeding* **Sergeant**

Duncan
    What bloody man is that? He can report,
    As seemeth by his plight, of the revolt
    The newest state.
Malcolm   This is the sergeant
    Who like a good and hardy soldier fought
    'Gainst my captivity. Hail, brave friend!   5
    Say to the King the knowledge of the broil
    As thou didst leave it.
Sergeant   Doubtful it stood,
    As two spent swimmers that do cling together
    And choke their art. The merciless Macdonwald
    Worthy to be a rebel, for to that   10
    The multiplying villainies of nature
    Do swarm upon him from – the Western Isles
    Of kernes and gallowglasses is supplied;
    And Fortune, on his damned quarrel smiling,
    Show'd like a rebel's whore. But all's too weak;   15
    For brave Macbeth – well he deserves that name –
    Disdaining Fortune, with his brandish'd steel
    Which smok'd with bloody execution,
    Like Valour's minion, carv'd out his passage
    Till he fac'd the slave;   20
    Which ne'er shook hands, nor bade farewell to him,
    Till he unseam'd him from the nave to th' chaps,
    And fix'd his head upon our battlements.
Duncan
    O valiant cousin! worthy gentleman!

A camp near Forres. This will be a military camp close to scene of the battle. It will also be near the moorland area where we have just seen the witches. **How do we know this?**

Alarum the trumpet's battle call.

1–3 *He can...state* Since he has clearly just been wounded, he should be able to give us up-to-date news of the battle.

5 *'Gainst my captivity* Earlier on this Sergeant had saved Malcolm from being captured.

6 *knowledge of the broil* information about the conflict.

8 *spent* exhausted.

9 *choke their art* prevent each other from swimming properly. Shakespeare compares the two opposing sides, Scotland and Norway, to two swimmers who are so tired that they cling to each other in exhaustion and therefore cannot fight. **What is he really suggesting about the state of the battle in this comparison?**

9–13 *The merciless...supplied* cruel Macdonwald, the rebel Scot, fit to be nothing but a traitor because of his numerous vices, had the additional support of wild Irish troops.

kernes light-armed foot-soldier.

gallowglasses horsemen armed with a sharp axe.

14–15 *Fortune...whore* Fortune smiles on Macdonwald's evil cause, like a prostitute, because she later bestows her favour on Macbeth. This is an example of personification (see glossary).

17 *Disdaining Fortune* Macbeth ignores Fortune and takes control over his own destiny.

17–18 *brandish'd...execution* Macbeth held out a sword still steaming with the hot blood of his most recent victim.

19 *minion* favourite. Valour, like Fortune, is here turned into a person.

carv'd out his passage cut his way through.

21 *which ne'er shook hands* Macbeth did not part with him.

22 *unseam'd...chaps* split him open (like a seam in a garment) from the navel to the jaw.

24 *cousin* Although Shakespeare uses the term for close friends rather than relatives, in fact Macbeth and Duncan were cousins. They were the sons of two sisters, and grandsons of the former King Malcolm.

Sergeant

As whence the sun gins his reflection   25
Shipwrecking storms and direful thunders break,
So from that spring whence comfort seem'd to come
Discomfort swells. Mark, King of Scotland, mark:
No sooner justice had, with valour arm'd,
Compell'd these skipping kernes to trust their heels,   30
But the Norweyan lord, surveying vantage,
With furbish'd arms and new supplies of men,
Began a fresh assault.

Duncan   Dismay'd not this
Our captains, Macbeth and Banquo?

Sergeant   Yes;
As sparrows eagles, or the hare the lion.   35
If I say sooth, I must report that they were
As cannons overcharg'd with double cracks;
So they doubly redoubled strokes upon the foe.
Except they meant to bathe in reeking wounds,
Or memorize another Golgotha,   40
I cannot tell –
But I am faint; my gashes cry for help.

Duncan

So well thy words become thee as thy wounds:
They smack of honour both. – Go get him surgeons.

The **Sergeant,** *with* **Attendants** *leave.*

Enter **Ross**

Who comes here?

Malcolm   The worthy Thane of Ross.   45

Lennox

What a haste looks through his eyes!
So should he look that seems to speak things strange.

Ross

God save the King!

Duncan

Whence cam'st thou, worthy thane?

Ross   From Fife, great King
Where the Norweyan banners flout the sky   50
And fan our people cold.

25–28 *As whence...discomfort swells* Although the east brings the rising sun, it also is the source of storms that cause shipwrecks. So, from a place you may think safe, danger can arise.

30 *compell'd....heels* made these unreliable soldiers run away.

31 *Norweyan lord* Sweno, king of Norway. (Norweyan is the old form of Norwegian.)

surveying vantage seeing an opportunity. The Scottish soldiers will probably relax and be easily caught off guard as they see the Irish run away.

32 *furbish'd arms* taking up new weapons.

35 *As sparrows...lion* The Sergeant suggests that Macbeth and Banquo were about as frightened of this second assault as an eagle is by a sparrow or a lion by a hare. **What tone of voice will the Sergeant use?**

36 *sooth* truth.

37 *double cracks* a double charge of gunpowder.

39–40 *Except....Golgotha* I am not sure whether they were intending to swim in blood or whether they wanted to make this scene as gory as the scene at Golgotha. Golgotha means the place of skulls and it was here that Christ was crucified. **What is the Sergeant really saying here about Macbeth and Banquo?**

43 both your words and your wounds do you credit.

44 *smack* taste, savour.

45 *Thane* the Scottish equivalent of a lord or a nobleman.

46–47 *What...strange* His expression suggests that he is in a hurry and his appearance that he has strange news to tell.

50 *flout* mock, scorn.

51 *fan our people cold* As the flags wave, men go cold with fear.

Norway himself, with terrible numbers,
Assisted by that most disloyal traitor,
The Thane of Cawdor, began a dismal conflict,
Till that Bellona's bridegroom, lapp'd in proof,   55
Confronted him with self-comparisons,
Point against point, rebellious arm 'gainst arm,
Curbing his lavish spirit; and to conclude,
The victory fell on us.

Duncan   Great happiness!

Ross

That now   60
Sweno, the Norways' king, craves composition;
Nor would we deign him burial of his men
Till he disbursed at Saint Colme's Inch,
Ten thousand dollars to our general use.

Duncan

No more that Thane of Cawdor shall deceive   65
Our bosom interest. Go pronounce his present death,
And with his former title greet Macbeth.

Ross

I'll see it done.

Duncan

What he hath lost, noble Macbeth hath won.

They go

52 *Norway himself* the King of Norway.

54 *dismal* doomed (for the Scots).

55 *Bellona's bridegroom* Bellona was the Roman goddess of war. **Who, therefore, is her bridegroom here?**

lapp'd in proof clad in strong, tested armour.

56–58 *Confronted...spirit* Macbeth showed the Thane of Cawdor that he was just as good a fighter both in body and in spirit. In doing this, he taught him a lesson for his insolence.

61 *craves composition* begs for peace.

62 *deign* allow.

63 *disbursed* paid.

Saint Colme's Inch This is now called Inchcomb. It is a small island in the Firth of Forth where there was an abbey dedicated to Saint Columba.

64 *dollars* These did not appear until 1518, five hundred years after the time of the action! It is quite probably a mistake on Shakespeare's part.

66 *our bosom interest* things of greatest importance to us.

present immediate.

POINTS TO CONSIDER

? How will Duncan, Malcolm, Donalbain and Lennox be dressed in this scene?

? *a bleeding Sergeant* Notice both here and later on in the scene how Shakespeare suggests the battle scene rather than showing it us directly. What reasons might he have had for doing this?

? 25–28 Although the Sergeant is simply thinking about the battle here, can you find anything ironic in his words? (See Irony in the section on Shakespeare's style)

ACT ONE SCENE 2 SUGGESTED ACTIVITIES

Production/Group Work

P1 Duncan has only a small but important part in the play. In groups, discuss your early impressions of him as a character. Then, as producers of the play, consider how you would allow his character to emerge in this scene.

P2 The Sergeant also has only a small part to play, but Shakespeare makes full use of him in this scene. Working in pairs, one person take on the role of the Sergeant and the other a news reporter. Conduct an interview in your own words. The character of the Sergeant as well as details of the battle should emerge.

Text

T1 Shakespeare introduces many pictures into his writing to make his ideas clearer. These are called *images*. (See section on Imagery on p 147). It is worth collecting these images because, when they are gathered together, they help you to get a clearer view of some of the more important themes in the play. Listed below are seven important *families* to which many of the images in the play belong.

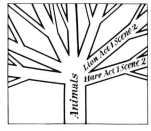

- NATURE AND NATURAL THINGS
- CLOTHES
- LIGHT AND DARKNESS
- ANIMALS
- DISEASE AND MEDICINE
- HUNTING/SPORT
- ACTING/THEATRE

Look at the drawing on the right.

It shows you how to build an IMAGE TREE. Draw seven trees and label each trunk with the seven families shown above. After most scenes you will be asked to pick out the images that you find and place them on branches of the appropriate Image Tree. Don't worry if you can't place every single image, but you will find that the seven trees cover many of the images you come across. Now look through scene 2 and add images to your trees as appropriate. Two have already been done for you in the drawing.

Written Work

W1 Write a report of the battle as it might be described on the television news. Read it aloud as a newsreader.

W2 Our early impression of Macbeth is formed here by what other people say about him. Write down five words that best describe him. Compare your words with someone else's and add to your list any words you had not thought of.

SCENE 3

An open place on a moor. Thunder.
Enter the three **Witches**

First Witch
Where hast thou been, sister?
Second Witch
Killing swine.
Third Witch
Sister, where thou?
First Witch
A sailor's wife had chestnuts in her lap,
And munch'd, and munch'd, and munch'd.   5
'Give me' quoth I.
'Aroint thee, witch!' the rump-fed ronyon cries.
Her husband's to Aleppo gone, master o'the Tiger;
But in a sieve I'll thither sail,
And like a rat without a tail,   10
I'll do, I'll do, and I'll do.
Second Witch
I'll give thee a wind.
First Witch
·Th'art kind.
Third Witch
And I another.
First Witch
I myself have all the other;   15
And the very ports they blow,
All the quarters that they know
I'the shipman's card.
I'll drain him dry as hay:
Sleep shall neither night nor day   20
Hang upon his pent-house lid;
He shall live a man forbid.
Weary sev'nights, nine times nine,
Shall he dwindle, peak, and pine:
Though his bark cannot be lost,   25

2 *killing swine* One of the many powers witches were said to possess was that of killing off by magic the animals of their enemies.
7 *Aroint thee* get lost!
7 *rump-fed* The sailor's wife perhaps lived on a diet of rump steak and would therefore be fat.
7 *ronyon* an insult, probably meaning something like *scabby* woman.
8 *Tiger* his ship's name.
9 *sieve* Witches were said to possess the unlikely power to sail the seas in a sieve! (See p 9).
10 *without a tail* **why?** (again see p 9.)
11 *do* this is repeated three times. **What does the First Witch really mean here?**
15–18 *I myself...card* The First Witch claims to control all the other winds on the points of the compass and to be able to make them blow out of any port. She can therefore ensure that the Tiger is kept stranded out at sea, unable to get in to safety.
21 *pent-house lid* A pent-house has a sloping roof something like an eyelid!
22 *forbid* put under a curse.
23 *weary sev'nights, nine times nine* that is, 81 weeks.
24 *dwindle, peak and pine* lose weight and waste away.
25 *cannot be lost* another limitation on the witches' powers. They can make ships leak, but not wreck them totally.

Yet it shall be tempest-tost.
Look what I have.

Second Witch
Show me, show me.

First Witch
Here I have a pilot's thumb,
Wreck'd as homeward he did come.   30

A drum beats within.

Third Witch
A drum! a drum!
Macbeth doth come.

All
The Weird Sisters, hand in hand,
Posters of the sea and land,
Thus do go about, about;   35
Thrice to thine, and thrice to mine,
And thrice again, to make up nine.
Peace! the charm's wound up.

Enter Macbeth *and* Banquo

Macbeth
So foul and fair a day I have not seen.

Banquo
How far is't call'd to Forres? What are these,   40
So wither'd, and so wild in their attire,
That look not like th'inhabitants o'th'earth,
And yet are on't? Live you, or are you ought
That man may question? You seem to understand me,
By each at once her choppy finger laying   45
Upon her skinny lips. You should be women,
And yet your beards forbid me to interpret
That you are so.

Macbeth   Speak if you can. What are you?

First Witch
All hail, Macbeth! hail to thee, Thane of Glamis!

Second Witch
All hail, Macbeth! hail to thee, Thane of Cawdor!   50

29 *pilot's thumb* **how might the witches use this**?
32 Macbeth is not yet visible. What powers do the witches show here?
33 *Weird* servants of destiny.
34 *posters* speedy travellers.
36–37 Magic numbers involving three.
38 *wound up* the spell is all ready. **What is the effect of Macbeth and Banquo entering at these words?**
40 *call'd* said to be.
43–44 *Live you...question* are you alive and can a man ask you questions?
45 *choppy* chapped. **Why do you think the witches are putting their fingers to their lips**?
50 *Thane of Cawdor* a good example of dramatic irony. (See notes on Irony on p 150.) The audience knows Macbeth was to receive this title.

Third Witch

    All hail, Macbeth! that shalt be King hereafter!

Banquo

    Good sir, why do you start, and seem to fear

    Things that do sound so fair? I'the name of truth,

    Are ye fantastical, or that indeed

    Which outwardly ye show? My noble partner   55

    You greet with present grace and great prediction

    Of noble having and of royal hope,

    That he seems rapt withal: to me you speak not.

    If you can look into the seeds of time

    And say which grain will grow and which will not,   60

    Speak then to me, who neither beg nor fear

    Your favours nor your hate.

First Witch

    Hail!

Second Witch

    Hail!

Third Witch

    Hail!   65

First Witch

    Lesser than Macbeth, and greater.

Second Witch

    Not so happy, yet much happier.

Third Witch

    Thou shalt get kings, though thou be none.

    So all hail, Macbeth and Banquo!

First Witch

    Banquo and Macbeth, all hail!   70

Macbeth

    Stay, you imperfect speakers, tell me more.

    By Sinel's death I know I am Thane of Glamis;

    But how of Cawdor? The Thane of Cawdor lives,

    A prosperous gentleman; and to be King

    Stands not within the prospect of belief,   75

    No more than to be Cawdor. Say from whence

    You owe this strange intelligence? or why

    Upon this blasted heath you stop our way

    With such prophetic greeting? Speak, I charge you.

51 *hereafter* some time in the future.

54 *fantastical* creation of the fancy.

56 *present grace* the title he possesses already (Glamis).

57 *noble having* of becoming Thane of Cawdor.

58 *rapt withal* lost to the world.

59 *look into the seeds of time* foresee what will happen. **Why does Shakespeare use the image of seeds to express this idea?**

68 *get kings* be the father of kings.

72 *Sinel* Macbeth's father, the former Thane of Glamis.

77 *owe* possess. *intelligence* information.

79 *I charge you* **what tone of voice does Macbeth use here?**

The **Witches** *vanish*

Banquo
The earth hath bubbles, as the water has,   80
And these are of them. Whither are they vanish'd?
Macbeth
Into the air; and what seem'd corporal melted
As breath into the wind. Would they had stay'd!
Banquo
Were such things here as we do speak about?
Or have we eaten on the insane root   85
That takes the reason prisoner?
Macbeth
Your children shall be kings.
Banquo   You shall be King.
Macbeth
And Thane of Cawdor too; went it not so?
Banquo
To the self-same tune and words. Who's here?

Enter **Ross** *and* **Angus**

Ross
The King hath happily receiv'd, Macbeth,   90
The news of thy success; and when he reads
Thy personal venture in the rebels' fight,
His wonders and his praises do contend
Which should be thine or his. Silenc'd with that,
In viewing o'er the rest o'the self-same day,   95
He finds thee in the stout Norweyan ranks,
Nothing afeard of what thyself didst make,
Strange images of death. As thick as hail
Came post with post, and every one did bear
Thy praises in his kingdom's great defence,   100
And pour'd them down before him.
Angus   We are sent
To give thee, from our royal master, thanks;
Only to herald thee into his sight,
Not pay thee.

80 *bubbles* Banquo is unsure whether these witches belong to the physical world or the supernatural world.
82 *corporal* physical.
83 *Would they had stay'd!* **What is Macbeth giving away about himself here?**
85–86 *insane root...prisoner* Hemlock or henbane are plants which, if eaten, caused madness.
87 *your children shall be kings* **Why does Macbeth say this?**
92 *personal venture* your own part in putting down the rebels.
93–94 *his wonders...or his* he is torn between astonishment at what Macbeth has done and admiration for him as a person.
97–98 *nothing afeard...death* Macbeth is not afraid of the sight of the bodies of those soldiers he has killed.
99 *post* messages.
101 *pour'd* carries on the image of hail.
103 *herald* escort.

Ross
    And, for an earnest of a greater honour,   105
    He bade me, from him, call thee Thane of Cawdor;
    In which addition, hail, most worthy Thane!
    For it is thine.
Banquo   What, can the Devil speak true?
Macbeth
    The Thane of Cawdor lives; why do you dress me
    In borrow'd robes?
Angus   Who was the Thane lives yet;   110
    But under heavy judgement bears that life
    Which he deserves to lose. Whether he was combin'd
    With those of Norway, or did line the rebel
    With hidden help and vantage, or that with both
    He labour'd in his country's wreck, I know not;   115
    But treasons capital, confess'd and prov'd.
    Have overthrown him.
Macbeth (*Aside*)   Glamis, and Thane of Cawdor:
    The greatest is behind. Thanks for your pains.
    (*Aside to* **Banquo**) Do you not hope your children
    shall be kings,
    When those that gave the Thane of Cawdor to me   120
    Promis'd no less to them?
Banquo (*Aside to* **Macbeth**) That, trusted home,
    Might yet enkindle you unto the crown,
    Besides the Thane of Cawdor. But 'tis strange,
    And oftentimes to win us to our harm,
    The instruments of darkness tell us truths,   125
    Win us with honest trifles, to betray's
    In deepest consequence. –
    Cousins, a word, I pray you.
Macbeth (*Aside*)   Two truths are told,
    As happy prologues to the swelling act
    Of the imperial theme. I thank you, gentlemen.   130
    (*Aside*) This supernatural soliciting
    Cannot be ill, cannot be good. If ill,
    Why hath it given me earnest of success,
    Commencing in a truth? I am Thane of Cawdor.
    If good, why do I yield to that suggestion   135

105 *for an earnest* as a down payment on.

108 *Devil* an important insight into Banquo's view of the Witches.

109–110 This is the first of many images in *Macbeth* that makes use of clothes. Shakespeare's contemporaries were extremely fashion-conscious and they could easily identify with the idea of ill-fitting or borrowed clothes.

111 *under heavy judgement* he has been sentenced to death.

112 *combin'd* in alliance.

113 *line the rebel* help Macdonwald.

115 *labour'd in his country's wreck* worked to destroy his country.

116 *treasons capital* treachery of a sort that deserves hanging.

119–121 *Do you not hope...them?* **What are Macbeth's real reasons for asking Banquo this question?**

121 *trusted home* if you believe in that completely.

122 *enkindle you* inspire you to try for the title of king.

123–127 *But 'tis strange...consequences* Banquo here points out how the Devil (instruments of darkness) sometimes lures us by small truths (honest trifles) in order to deceive us in really serious matters and ultimately destroy us. Bear these lines in mind as the action progresses for in many ways they are a summary of the whole play.

128–142 These lines, spoken aside by Macbeth, are the first example of a soliloquy. (See Glossary). Although it might seem strange to us that at this moment Macbeth should speak his thoughts aloud, to Shakespeare's audience, it would seem a natural way for a character to try to come to terms with a problem. Here, therefore, as in other soliloquies, we find Macbeth looking at both sides of the question and trying to work towards a solution. Through the soliloquy, we can share his dilemma.

129–130 *As happy...imperial theme* Using the image of a play, Macbeth implies that becoming Thane of Glamis and Cawdor were merely introductions (prologues) to the great climax of the play, namely himself becoming king (imperial theme).

131 *supernatural soliciting* the forces of the supernatural urging him to act.

133 *earnest* assurance.

135 *suggestion* **what does this refer to?**

Whose horrid image doth unfix my hair
And make my seated heart knock at my ribs
Against the use of nature? Present fears
Are less than horrible imaginings.
My thought, whose murder yet is but fantastical,   140
Shakes so my single state of man
That function is smother'd in surmise,
And nothing is but what is not.

Banquo
Look how our partner's rapt.

Macbeth (*Aside*)
If chance will have me King, why, chance may crown me,   145
Without my stir.

Banquo   New honours come upon him,
Like our strange garments, cleave not to their mould
But with the aid of use.

Macbeth (*Aside*)   Come what come may,
Time and the hour runs through the roughest day.

Banquo
Worthy Macbeth, we stay upon your leisure.   150

Macbeth
Give me your favour: my dull brain was wrought
With things forgotten. Kind gentlemen, your pains
Are registered where every day I turn
The leaf to read them. Let us toward the King.
(*Aside to* **Banquo**) Think upon what hath chanc'd; and,
at more time,   155
The interim having weigh'd it, let us speak
Our free hearts each to other.

Banquo (*Aside to* **Macbeth**) Very gladly.

Macbeth (*Aside to* **Banquo**)
Till then, enough. – Come, friends.

They leave together.

136–138 *horrid image...nature* This horrifying picture makes my hair stand on end and my heart thump unnaturally against my rib cage.

138–139 *present fears...imaginings* A fear that is in the mind can be far more dreadful than a real fear.

140 *fantastical* imaginary.

142–143 *function...surmise* Macbeth is so dominated by thoughts of murder that he has lost the power to act (function) and the only things that seem real are in his imagination.

144 *rapt* lost in thought.

146 *without my stir* he might become king in the natural course of events since he is a member of the royal family. (Macbeth was cousin to King Duncan.)

146–148 Banquo compares the strangeness of the new title Macbeth has acquired to the strangeness of new clothes which haven't yet shaped themselves to our body. This would again mean more to Shakespeare's contemporaries whose clothes would all be made by hand to fit them individually.

149 *Time...day* even the most difficult day comes to an end. **What impression does Macbeth give here of his intentions?**

150 *leisure* we're waiting for you! **How must Macbeth's behaviour appear to the others at this moment?**

151 *My dull brain...forgotten* my mind was on something else.

152–154 *Kind gentlemen...them* Macbeth suggests here that all the services these men have rendered him are written in a book he reads each day. A very complicated way of saying 'thank you'! **Is there any reason why Macbeth should speak in such a laboured way?**

156 *The interim...it* when we've both had time to think it over. **What impression do you get here of Macbeth's words to Banquo?**

POINTS TO CONSIDER

? What expectations will the appearance of the witches create in the audience this time? Think back to their words in the first scene.

? 39 *foul...fair* Where have we already heard these words? An earlier impression concerning the relationship between Macbeth and the Witches should now be confirmed.

? 45 Notice the series of questions from Banquo. He is uncertain about the witches from the beginning. What is Macbeth's attitude to them?

? 49–51 How does Macbeth react to the Witches' greetings and what is now passing through his mind?

? 54–55 Banquo is very aware of the possibility that the outside appearance of things might be very deceptive. What does this suggest about his character?

? 89 *tune and words* Why do you think Macbeth describes the Witches' words in this way?

? 101 What do we learn of Macbeth's character from Ross's words here?

? 138–139 Do you agree with this suggestion?

ACT ONE SCENE 3 SUGGESTED ACTIVITIES

Production/Group Work

P1 Macbeth and Banquo both react to the Witches differently. If you were producing the play, you would need to show this in ways other than just words. In groups of three, discuss lines 39 to 89 and 117 to 158. Make notes on how these lines might be performed concentrating on the different reactions of Macbeth and Banquo. Consider in particular how to deal with the stage directions 'aside'. Then try acting out these lines.

Text

T1a) Here is a three-part exercise designed to make you aware of Shakespeare's choice of words. Re-read Macbeth's soliloquy, lines 128 to 143. Then, working in pairs and without the text, fill in the words missing from the speech below. (Write your words in a list on a separate sheet of paper, not in the book.) Try to use Shakespeare's original words if you can remember them. If not, use words that seem appropriate to you.

Two truths are told,
As happy prologue to the _____ act
Of the _____ theme. I thank you, gentlemen.
This _____ soliciting
Cannot be _____, cannot be _____. If ill,

Why hath it given me earnest of _____,
Commencing in a _____? I am Thane of Cawdor.
If, good, why do I _____to that suggestion
Whose _____image doth _____ my hair
And make my seated heart _____ at my ribs
Against the use of nature. Present _____
Are less than horrible
My thought, whose _____ yet is but fantastical,
_____ so my single state of man
That function is _____ in surmise,
And nothing is but what is _____.

b) When you have finished, look at the speech in the text and write down the original words in a list next to your own. Now, with your partner, compare the two lists of words. If you have used different words, discuss with your partner what effect Shakespeare's words convey and how they are different from yours. This might involve the meaning of the word. It might also involve the rhythm or the way in which images are used (See 'Shakespeare's Style' p 145)

c) Now, working on your own and using Shakespeare's original words (from your second list) write down briefly what they suggest about Macbeth's state of mind.

T2 Add more images from this scene to your Image Trees.

Written Work

W1 This is an important scene for our understanding of Macbeth's character. Write up an entry for his diary for this day. In this he should reveal his innermost thoughts and feelings and his true reactions to the Witches and their prophecies.

W2 Write a similar entry in a diary for Banquo concentrating on his reaction to the Witches and anything odd he notices about Macbeth's behaviour.

W3 Write two horoscopes or predictions in the style of the Witches. One could be for yourself and one for someone famous.

SCENE 4

Forres. A room in the palace.
Flourish. Enter **Duncan, Malcolm, Donalbain, Lennox** *and* **Attendants**

Duncan
    Is execution done on Cawdor? Are not
    Those in commission yet return'd?
Malcolm   My liege,
    They are not yet come back. But I have spoke
    With one that saw him die; who did report
    That very frankly he confess'd his treasons   5
    Implor'd your Highness' pardon, and set forth
    A deep repentance. Nothing in his life
    Became him like the leaving it; he died
    As one that had been studied in his death,
    To throw away the dearest thing he ow'd   10
    As 'twere a careless trifle.
Duncan   There's no art
    To find the mind's construction in the face.
    He was a gentleman on whom I built
    An absolute trust.

             Enter **Macbeth, Banquo, Ross** *and* **Angus**

            O worthiest cousin!
    The sin of my ingratitude even now   15
    Was heavy on me. Thou art so far before
    That swiftest wing of recompense is slow
    To overtake thee. Would thou hadst less deserv'd,
    That the proportion both of thanks and payment
    Might have been mine! Only I have left to say,   20
    More is thy due than more than all can pay.
Macbeth
    The service and the loyalty I owe,
    In doing it, pays itself. Your Highness' part
    Is to receive our duties; and our duties
    Are to your throne and state, children and servants; 25
    Which do but what they should by doing everything

We now move inside the palace of King Duncan. The whole occasion has an air of formality, in contrast to the previous scenes. The King and his courtiers might be richly dressed.

Flourish the arrival of the King is announced by a fanfare of trumpets.
2 *in commission* in charge of the execution of Cawdor.
9 *studied* rehearsed or practised. Duncan compares the courageous way in which Cawdor faced death to an actor well rehearsed in the art of 'dying'.
11 *careless* trivial, worthless.
11–12 You can never learn how to judge what a man is really like by looking at his face.
At this moment, Macbeth appears. What effect does Shakespeare create by this?
16–18 *Thou art so far...thee* Duncan suggests here that there is a race going on between Macbeth's worth and his own gratitude. Macbeth's worth is leading in the race and Duncan's gratitude is having problems catching up!
20–21 *Only...can pay* I can't thank you enough. Both Duncan and Macbeth are excessively polite to each other, as would have been appropriate in the court.
23 *pays itself* is its own reward.
26–27 *Which do...honour* We're only doing our duty by protecting your love and honour.

Safe toward your love and honour.

Duncan Welcome hither.
I have begun to plant thee, and will labour
To make thee full of growing. Noble Banquo,
That hast no less deserv'd, nor must be known 30
No less to have done so, let me infold thee,
And hold thee to my heart.

Banquo There if I grow,
The harvest is your own.

Duncan My plenteous joys,
Wanton in fulness, seek to hide themselves
In drops of sorrow. Sons, kinsmen, thanes, 35
And you whose places are the nearest, know
We will establish our estate upon
Our eldest, Malcolm, whom we name hereafter
The Prince of Cumberland; which honour must
Not unaccompanied invest him only, 40
But signs of nobleness, like stars, shall shine
On all deservers. From hence to Inverness,
And bind us further to you.

Macbeth
The rest is labour, which is not us'd for you.
I'll be myself the harbinger, and make joyful 45
The hearing of my wife with your approach;
So humbly take my leave.

Duncan My worthy Cawdor!

Macbeth (*Aside*)
The Prince of Cumberland! That is a step,
On which I must fall down, or else o'er-leap,
For in my way it lies. Stars, hide your fires! 50
Let not light see my black and deep desires.
The eye wink at the hand; yet let that be
Which the eye fears, when it is done, to see.

He goes

28–29 *I have...growing* Duncan sees himself as a gardener sowing seeds and nurturing them. In this way, he assumes the role of guardian to Macbeth, bestowing titles on him and encouraging his personal development.
32 Banquo extends Duncan's earlier image.
34 *wanton* overflowing. Duncan can't stop crying for joy.
36 *nearest* to the throne.
37 Notice Duncan changes here from *I* to *we*, the royal plural. **How does this affect the atmosphere in court?**
39 *The Prince of Cumberland.* Cumberland was originally part of Scotland. The title was equivalent to the Prince of Wales today, (ie given to the heir to the throne). Unlike today, the title of king did not automatically pass down to the eldest son. The king could choose his successor from any of his relatives.
39–42 *which honour...deservers* Duncan will confer honours not only on his son but on all deserving men.
42 *Inverness* Macbeth's castle.
44 *The rest...you* it's only hard work when it's not for a king. **How could you describe Macbeth's tone here?**
50 *Stars, hide your fires!* **What is Macbeth really afraid of?**
52–53 *The eye...to see* don't let my eye see what my hand is doing, but do let my hand carry out the deed my eye is afraid of seeing! Macbeth wants the evil deed done without having to face the consequences.
54 *he* Macbeth. It seems likely that in the course of the soliloquy Banquo has been talking to Duncan of Macbeth's qualities. Duncan is here agreeing with him.

Duncan
        True, worthy Banquo; he is full so valiant;
        And in his commendations I am fed;   55
        It is a banquet to me. Let's after him,
        Whose care is gone before to bid us welcome.
        It is a peerless kinsman.

                        Flourish. They leave

55–56 *in his commendations...to me* Duncan suggests that compliments about Macbeth are like fine food to him. **This is another example of dramatic irony. Why?**

58 *peerless* without equal.

POINT TO CONSIDER

? We have only seen Duncan in the context of battle scenes so far. How does the formality of this court scene affect our impression of him?

ACT ONE SCENE 4 SUGGESTED ACTIVITIES

Production/Group Work

P1 Although we have already met Duncan in scene 2, only here do we begin to see what he is really like as a king. In groups, discuss his character and then work out how, as producer, you will portray him in this scene. Consider his age, costume, his bearing, how he speaks, his relationship with different characters, particularly Macbeth.

P2 We now see Macbeth contemplating murder. Using the evidence of the last scene and this one, discuss in groups Macbeth's character and the likelihood of his carrying out the crime. It does not matter whether you know what happens or not but limit the discussion to the evidence of the two scenes.

Text

T1 Macbeth's second soliloquy (lines 48 – 53) is spoken in response to the news that Malcolm has been named as heir to the throne. What does Macbeth reveal about himself in this speech?

T2 Add more images to your Image Trees.

Written Work

W1 Throughout this scene, Donalbain, Duncan's younger son, has been an onlooker. Imagine the whole scene from his point of view, then write a conversation between him and his brother Malcolm in which he expresses some concern about Macbeth. Portray Malcolm as you feel is appropriate. He may have had his own suspicions, or he may have noticed nothing.

SCENE 5

Inverness. A room in Macbeth's castle.
Enter **Lady Macbeth**, *reading a letter.*

Lady Macbeth
 'They met me in the day of success; and I have learn'd by
 the perfect'st report they have more in them than mortal
 knowledge. When I burn'd in desire to question them
 further, they made themselves air, into which they
 vanish'd. Whiles I stood rapt in the wonder of it,   5
 came missives from the King, who all-hailed me "Thane of
 Cawdor"; by which title, before, these weird sisters
 saluted me, and referr'd me to the coming on of time, with
 "Hail, king that shalt be!" This have I thought good to
 deliver thee, my dearest partner of greatness, that   10
 thou mightst not lose the dues of rejoicing, by being
 ignorant of what greatness is promis'd thee. Lay it to
 thy heart, and farewell.'
 Glamis thou art, and Cawdor; and shalt be
 What thou art promis'd. Yet I do fear thy nature;   15
 It is too full o'the milk of human kindness
 To catch the nearest way. Thou wouldst be great;
 Art not without ambition, but without
 The illness should attend it; what thou wouldst highly,
 That wouldst thou holily; wouldst not play false,   20
 And yet wouldst wrongly win. Thou'dst have, great Glamis,
 That which cries 'Thus thou must do' if thou have it;
 And that which rather thou dost fear to do
 Than wishest should be undone. Hie thee hither,
 That I may pour my spirits in thine ear,   25
 And chastise with the valour of my tongue
 All that impedes thee from the golden round
 Which fate and metaphysical aid doth seem
 To have thee crown'd withal.

Enter a **Messenger**

 What is your tidings?

From the interior of Duncan's castle in the previous scene, we now move to Macbeth's castle and to Lady Macbeth, who stands reading a letter from her husband.

1–13 So far the play has been written in poetry. This letter is written in prose, the normal language of written and spoken English.
1 *They met me...* Lady Macbeth is clearly well into the letter. **What effect does Shakespeare create by beginning the scene in this way**?
2 *perfect'st report* Macbeth has had proof that the witches are speaking the truth from the fact that the Cawdor prophecy has come true.
4–5 *made themselves air...vanish'd* This should have been a hint to Macbeth that they were witches. (See notes on the Weird Sisters p 9).
5 *rapt* amazed.
6 *missives* messengers.
8 *coming on of time* future.
10 *deliver* report to.
11 *dues of rejoicing* your share of the joy.
14–15 *and shalt be...promised* Lady Macbeth states here that Macbeth will be king.
16 *milk of human kindness* Milk is seen here (and elsewhere) as an image of kindness, sweetness and goodness. It also belongs to the natural world.
19 *The illness should attend it* Macbeth has not got the evil nature that goes with ambition.
19–20 *what thou wouldst...holily* You would like to be King (highest ambition) but by fair means not foul.
21 *wrongly win* achieve what does not belong to you.
21–24 *Thou'ds have ...undone* you want the crown for which you must commit murder. Even though you're afraid to murder him, you'd be quite happy for it to be done by someone else.
24 *Hie thee hither* hurry home to me.
26 *chastise* thrash or drive away.
27 *golden round* crown.
28 *fate and metaphysical aid* chance and the powers of the supernatural, ie the witches.

Messenger

    The King comes here tonight.

Lady Macbeth   Thou'rt mad to say it.   30

    Is not thy master with him? who, were't so,

    Would have inform'd for preparation.

Messenger

    So please you, it is true: our Thane is coming.

    One of my fellows had the speed of him,

    Who, almost dead for breath, had scarcely more   35

    Than would make up his message.

Lady Macbeth   Give him tending:

    He brings great news.

*   The messenger goes*

                The raven himself is hoarse

    That croaks the fatal entrance of Duncan

    Under my battlements. Come you spirits

    That tend on mortal thoughts, unsex me here;   40

    And fill me, from the crown to the toe, top-full

    Of direst cruelty. Make thick my blood,

    Stop up th'access and passage to remorse,

    That no compunctious visitings of nature

    Shake my fell purpose nor keep peace between   45

    Th'effect and it. Come to my woman's breasts,

    And take my milk for gall, you murd'ring ministers,

    Wherever in your sightless substances

    You wait on nature's mischief. Come, thick night,

    And pall thee in the dunnest smoke of hell,   50

    That my keen knife see not the wound it makes,

    Nor heaven peep through the blanket of the dark

    To cry 'Hold, hold'.

*   Enter* Macbeth

                Great Glamis! Worthy Cawdor!

    Greater than both, by the all-hail hereafter!

    Thy letters have transported me beyond   55

    This ignorant present, and I feel now

    The future in the instant.

30 *Thou'rt mad to say it* **Why does Lady Macbeth react like this and what does she give away about herself?**

32 *inform'd for preparation* let us know in advance so that we could prepare.

34 *had the speed of him* travelled faster than him.

35–36 *had scarcely more...message* he was so out of breath he could scarcely deliver his message.

36 *tending* take care of him.

37 *raven...hoarse* The raven is said to bring bad luck. At this moment, the bird croaks even more hoarsely than usual and Lady Macbeth compares its croak to the breathless message from the messenger. Both announcements she sees as fatal to Duncan.

39 *my battlements* **What is the effect of** *my*?

39–40 *Come you...thoughts* Lady Macbeth calls upon destructive spirits or those associated with death.

40–41 *unsex me here...cruelty* she wants all her natural and normal, womanly qualities to be replaced by an unnatural, cruel, ruthless disposition. **What does this suggest about the way Lady Macbeth sees her own character? What truth does she recognise in herself?**

42–43 *Make thick...remorse* she asks that her blood should be thickened so that sorrow cannot pass along her veins to her heart.

44 *compunctious visitings of nature* pricking of her conscience.

45 *fell* cruel, wicked.

45–46 *keep peace...it* come between my plot and its successful execution.

47 *gall* bitter liquid.

47 *murd'ring ministers* the spirits mentioned in line 39.

48 *sightless substances* invisible forms.

49 *wait on nature's mischief* ready to join in carrying out any evil deeds.

50 *pall* shroud. *dunnest* darkest.

Macbeth enters. How will he and his wife greet each other? What tone of voice will Lady Macbeth use to speak to Macbeth?

54 *all-hail hereafter* future prophecy.

56 *ignorant* because it knows nothing of the future.

57 *future in the instant* as though it has already happened. **What does she really mean?**

Macbeth   My dearest love,
Duncan comes here to-night.
Lady Macbeth   And when goes hence?
Macbeth
Tomorrow, as he purposes.
Lady Macbeth   O, never
Shall sun that morrow see!   60
Your face, my thane, is as a book where men
May read strange matters. To beguile the time,
Look like the time; bear welcome in your eye,
Your hand, your tongue; look like th'innocent flower,
But be the serpent under't. He that's coming   65
Must be provided for; and you shall put
This night's great business into my dispatch;
Which shall to all our nights and days to come
Give solely sovereign sway and masterdom.
Macbeth
We will speak further.
Lady Macbeth   Only look up clear;   70
To alter favour ever is to fear.
Leave all the rest to me.

They go

62 *beguile* deceive.
63 *look like the time* adopt an appropriate expression.
64–65 *innocent flower...serpent under't* **What does this mean?**
67 *dispatch* hands, management.
68–69 The result of tonight's business means that we shall be no less than King (and Queen) of Scotland for the rest of our lives.
69 How does Macbeth react to Lady Macbeth's confident predictions?
70 *clear* with a look of innocence.
71 *To alter...fear* if you change the expression on your face, it will prove your fear and guilt.

POINTS TO CONSIDER

? 1–13 Why do you think that Shakespeare has written the letter in prose? (See notes on Shakespeare's use of verse and prose, p 146).

? 14–15 What tone (see p 149) does Lady Macbeth use in these lines? It may help to read the lines aloud.

? 19 This is an important statement about ambition. Do you believe, as Shakespeare seems to suggest, that to reach the highest positions in life, people must be in some way abnormal?

? 49–53 Macbeth says something very like this elsewhere in the play. Where?

? 64–65 Does this image give you a clear picture of what Lady Macbeth is saying? Notice the way it reinforces an important theme we have already come across, that the outside appearance of something may give a false impression of what it is like on the inside.

? 71 What is your impression of Macbeth and Lady Macbeth here at the end of the scene?

ACT ONE SCENE 5 SUGGESTED ACTIVITIES

Production/Group Work

P1 This is the first time we have met Lady Macbeth. In groups, discuss the sort of person she is and then choose *five* adjectives that best sum her up.

P2 Working in pairs, modernise this scene by taking on the roles of a 20th-century husband and wife who have just been re-united after some time apart. Work out your own details, but try to reflect the events and the characters of this scene.

Text

T1a) Here is a three -part exercise designed to make you aware of Shakespeare's choice of words. Re-read Lady Macbeth's soliloquy, lines 39–53, 'Come you spirits....hold.' Then, working in pairs and without the text, fill in the words missing from the speech below. (Write your words in a list on a separate piece of paper, not in the book) Try to use Shakespeare's original words if you can remember them. If not, use words that seem appropriate to you.

Come, you _____
That tend on _____ thoughts, _____ me here;
And fill me, from the _____ to the _____, top-full
Of direst _____. Make thick my _____,
Stop up th'access and passage to _____,
That no compunctious visitings of _____
Shake my _____ purpose nor keep peace between
Th' effect and it. Come to my woman's _____,
And take my milk for _____, you murdering ministers,
Wherever in your sightless _____
You wait on nature's _____. Come, thick _____,
And _____ thee in the dunnest _____ of _____,
That my keen _____ see not the _____ it makes,
Nor heaven peep through the blanket of the _____
To cry '_____, _____'.

b) Look at the speech in the text and write down the original words in a list next to your own. With your partner, compare the two lists of words. If you have used different words, discuss with your partner what effect Shakespeare's words convey and how they are different from yours. This might involve the meaning of the word. It might also involve the rhythm of the words or the way in which images are used. (See Shakespeare's Style p 145).

c) Lady Macbeth is trying to move out of the world she knows into another one. Working on your own and using as many of Shakespeare's original words as possible (from your second list) write a sentence or two to describe the world Lady Macbeth hopes to move into.

T2 Add more images to your Image Trees.

Written Work

W1 In the course of this scene Macbeth has been making his way home. Describe his thoughts during the journey.

SCENE 6

Inverness. Outside Macbeth's castle.
Hautboys and torches. Enter **Duncan, Malcolm, Donalbain, Banquo,**
Lennox, Macduff, Ross, Angus *and* **Attendants.**

Duncan
This castle hath a pleasant seat; the air
Nimbly and sweetly recommends itself
Unto our gentle senses.
Banquo   This guest of summer,
The temple-haunting martlet, does approve
By his lov'd mansionry, that the heaven's breath   5
Smells wooingly here: no jutty, frieze,
Buttress, nor coign of vantage, but this bird
Hath made her pendent bed and procreant cradle.
Where they most breed and haunt, I have observ'd
The air is delicate.

Enter **Lady Macbeth**

Duncan   See, see, our honour'd hostess!   10
The love that follows us sometime is our trouble,
Which still we thank as love. Herein I teach you
How you shall bid God 'ild us for your pains,
And thank us for your trouble.
Lady Macbeth   All our service
In every point twice done, and then done double,   15
Were poor and single business to contend

For this scene the action moves to the outside of Macbeth's castle. Notice the group of loyal supporters who arrive with Duncan – his sons, Malcolm and Donalbain and other noble relatives.

Hautboys oboes.
Torches the attendants have come out of the castle carrying these torches, suggesting that it is very dark inside, despite the fact that it is light outside.
1 *seat* setting.
3 *gentle senses* our senses soothed or made gentle by the pleasant air.
guest the bird migrates in winter and is therefore a summer visitor.
4 *martlet* a house martin that often builds its nest in a church. **Compare this with the raven of the previous scene.**
approve prove.
5 *mansionary* building.
6–7 *jutty, frieze, Buttress* these are all projecting parts of a building.
7 *coign of vantage* convenient corner.
8 *pendent bed* the bird has built a hanging nest.
procreant for the young birds.
11–14 Duncan jokes here with Lady Macbeth. He suggests that he is helping her to become a better person by his visit. The inconvenience he causes her will eventually be rewarded by God.
14–18 Lady Macbeth answers in a similar manner. If she had to do everything four times over, she says, it would still not add up to the honour the King brings by staying at her house.

Against those honours deep and broad, wherewith
Your Majesty loads our house; for those of old,
And the late dignities heap'd up to them,
We rest your hermits.

Duncan   Where's the Thane of Cawdor?   20
We cours'd him at the heels, and had a purpose
To be his purveyor; but he rides well,
And his great love, sharp as his spur, hath holp him
To his home before us. Fair and noble hostess,
We are your guest tonight.

Lady Macbeth   Your servants ever   25
Have theirs, themselves, and what is theirs, in compt,
To make their audit at your Highness' pleasure,
Still to return your own.

Duncan   Give me your hand;
Conduct me to mine host: we love him highly,
And shall continue our graces towards him.   30
By your leave, hostess.

They go in

18 *those of old* honours previously bestowed.
19 *late dignities* possibly making Macbeth Thane of Cawdor.
20 *hermits* we shall offer up prayers for you.
21 *cours'd him at the heels* chased him closely.
22 *purveyor* the official who prepares the king's reception.
25–28 Your servants have their own servants, themselves and all that belongs to them, all available for your pleasure. They are ready to give to you what is really your own. Lady Macbeth uses an image from accounting here (*in compt, make audit*) to suggest the relationship between king and subjects. Just as an accountant manages money that belongs to someone else, so the subjects of the King have servants who must be given to the King for his own use whenever necessary.
31 *By your leave* Duncan, according to custom, would probably kiss Lady Macbeth as he takes her hand. **What would be the effect of this upon the audience?**

POINT TO CONSIDER

? 14–20 Does Lady Macbeth give away anything about herself during this speech? What expression will she have on her face? Will anyone present notice anything different about her?

ACT ONE SCENE 6 SUGGESTED ACTIVITIES

Production/Group Work

P1 How would you, as producers, provide the setting for this scene? Work in pairs.

P2 This is the last time we see Duncan on stage. The producer of the play will want to leave a clear impression on the audience of the sort of man Duncan is. In groups of three, discuss and agree upon your interpretation of the man. Then take on the roles of Duncan, Lady Macbeth and the producer and produce and act out line 10 to the end of the scene.

Text

T1 Re-read the first ten lines of the scene. Then, work in pairs and consider what impression they give of the outside of Macbeth's castle. What contrasts are made with what we know of the inside? What theme within the play does this contrast re-inforce?

T2 Add more images to your Image Trees.

Written Work

W1 Choose any one of the onlookers of this scene and write down what they might be thinking.

SCENE 7

A room in Macbeth's castle.
Hautboys and torches. Enter Servants carrying dishes for a feast. Then
enter **Macbeth**

Macbeth
   If it were done when 'tis done, then 'twere well
   It were done quickly. If th'assassination
   Could trammel up the consequence, and catch,
   With his surcease, success; that but this blow
   Might be the be-all and the end-all. Here,   5
   But here upon this bank and shoal of time,
   We'd jump the life to come. But in these cases
   We still have judgement here, that we but teach
   Bloody instructions, which being taught return
   To plague th'inventor. This even-handed justice   10
   Commends th'ingredience of our poison'd chalice
   To our own lips. He's here in double trust:

Now we are back in Macbeth's castle. The numerous torches indicate the depth of darkness inside.
Macbeth enters alone and, in his soliloquy, shows us his dilemma. **What will probably have happened since we last saw him?**

1 *done* If the murder were over and done with, then the sooner the better.

3 *trammel up* entangle in a net.

4 *surcease* its conclusion. Macbeth compares the assassin to someone laying a bird trap and he wishes that, using his net, he could control the outcome as well as catch the bird.

5 *be all . . . here* all that is needed to end everything.

6 *bank and shoal of time* Macbeth sees life as a sandbank in a shallow place surrounded by a sea of eternity.

7 *jump* risk, that is, life after death.

8–10 We give lessons in murder. Our violence, through retaliation, then comes back to torment us.

10 *even-handed* fair-minded.

11–12 *commends . . . lips* means that we ourselves should drink the poison that we have given to another.

12 *double trust* a) as a relative and a subject b) as a host.

First, as I am his kinsman and his subject,
Strong both against the deed; then, as his host,
Who should against his murderer shut the door,   15
Not bear the knife myself. Besides, this Duncan
Hath borne his faculties so meek, hath been
So clear in his great office, that his virtues
Will plead like angels, trumpet-tongu'd, against
The deep damnation of his taking-off;   20
And Pity, like a naked new-born babe,
Striding the blast, or heaven's Cherubin hors'd
Upon the sightless couriers of the air,
Shall blow the horrid deed in every eye,
That tears shall drown the wind. I have no spur   25
To prick the sides of my intent, but only
Vaulting ambition, which o'er-leaps itself,
And falls on th'other.

Enter Lady Macbeth

                    How now! What news?

Lady Macbeth
    He has almost supp'd. Why have you left the chamber?
Macbeth
    Hath he ask'd for me?
Lady Macbeth Know you not he has?   30
Macbeth
    We will proceed no further in this business.
    He hath honour'd me of late; and I have bought
    Golden opinions from all sorts of people,
    Which would be worn now in their newest gloss,
    Not cast aside so soon.
Lady Macbeth   Was the hope drunk   35
    Wherein you dress'd yourself? Hath it slept since,
    And wakes it now to look so green and pale
    At what it did so freely? From this time
    Such I account thy love. Art thou afeard
    To be the same in thine own act and valour   40
    As thou art in desire? Wouldst thou have that
    Which thou esteem'st the ornament of life,

14 *strong both* both strong reasons.
17 *Hath borne . . . meek* he has used his kingly powers humbly.
18 *clear* clear of blame.
20 *taking-off* murder. Macbeth finds it difficult to use the actual word *murder*. Instead here, and elsewhere, he makes use of an euphemism — that is, a mild substitute for the word, one that sounds less ugly than *murder*.
21–25 Macbeth imagines that because Duncan is such a virtuous man, his crimes against him will be made known to the whole world.
22 *striding the blast* Pity is seen as a baby riding on the winds.
22 *Cherubin* an angel.
23 *sightless couriers of the air* wind. The angel is also seen as riding the winds but on a horse.
24 *shall blow . . . eye* will make the deed known to everyone.
25–28 Macbeth now acknowledges that his ambition is evil. He compares his ambition to a young man on a horse who tries to jump too high and ends up falling on the other side of the obstacle himself.
29 What do you think is Lady Macbeth's real reason for following Macbeth out of the chamber?
31 What tone of voice does Macbeth now use?
32 Macbeth compares the good opinion he now has from many people to new clothes which he wants to enjoy wearing.
35 Notice how Lady Macbeth outdoes her husband in tone.
36 *dress'd* Lady Macbeth takes up Macbeth's clothes image and introduces the idea of drunkenness. She compares Macbeth's original confidence to drunkenness and suggests that he is now waking up with a hangover and unable to carry out his original plan.
39 *Such I account thy love* **what does she mean?**
39–41 Lady Macbeth asks whether he is afraid to carry out what he wants to do.
41–43 *Wouldst . . . esteem* can you be ambitious for the crown and yet remain a coward by not carrying out the deed?

And live a coward in thine own esteem,
Letting 'I dare not' wait upon 'I would',
Like the poor cat i'th'adage?

Macbeth   Prithee, peace;   45
I dare do all that may become a man;
Who dares do more is none.

Lady Macbeth   What beast was't then
That made you break this enterprise to me?
When you durst do it, then you were a man;
And to be more than what you were, you would   50
Be so much more the man. Nor time nor place
Did then adhere, and yet you would make both:
They have made themselves, and that their fitness now
Does unmake you. I have given suck, and know
How tender 'tis to love the babe that milks me: 55
I would, while it was smiling in my face,
Have pluck'd my nipple from his boneless gums,
And dash'd the brains out, had I so sworn
As you have done to this.

Macbeth   If we should fail?

Lady Macbeth
We fail?   60
But screw your courage to the sticking place,
And we'll not fail. When Duncan is asleep,
Whereto the rather shall his day's hard journey
Soundly invite him, his two chamberlains
Will I with wine and wassail so convince   65
That memory, the warder of the brain,
Shall be a fume, and the receipt of reason
A limbeck only. When in swinish sleep
Their drenched natures lie as in a death,
What cannot you and I perform upon   70
Th' unguarded Duncan? what not put upon
His spongy officers, who shall bear the guilt
Of our great quell?

Macbeth   Bring forth men-children only;
For thy undaunted mettle should compose
Nothing but males. Will it not be receiv'd,   75

44 *adage* proverb. She is referring to the proverb 'The cat would eat fish, but would not wet her feet'.
46 *become* be fitting for.
48 *break . . . mention* **What further information does this give the audience?**
50–51 *And . . . man* by being even more brave than you were then, you would be even more of a man.
51–54 *Nor time . . . you* neither the time nor the place were then suitable, yet you were prepared to find them. Now they are suitable, you're afraid to take advantage of them.
59 *If we should fail?* **What effect have Lady Macbeth's words had on Macbeth?**
60 *We fail?* **What does she really mean by this?**
61 *But . . . place* she asks Macbeth to screw up his courage (like a tuning peg on a musical instrument) until it is taut and won't budge.
64 *chamberlains* bodyguards.
65 *wassail* merrymaking. *convince* overpower.
67 *fume* fog. *receipt* container.
68 *limbeck* a distilling flask.
69 *drenched* drunken.
72 *spongy* drunken.
73 *quell* murder.
74 *mettle* courage.
75 *receiv'd* believed, accepted.

When we have mark'd with blood those sleepy two
Of his own chamber, and us'd their very daggers,
That they have done't?

Lady Macbeth   Who dares receive it other,
As we shall make our griefs and clamour roar
Upon his death?

Macbeth   I am settled, and bend up   80
Each corporal agent to this terrible feat.
Away, and mock the time with fairest show;
False face must hide what the false heart doth know.

They go out.

79–80 *As . . . death* we shall cry out with so much grief and noise when we learn of his death.
80 *bend up* make ready.
81 *corporal agent* all the powers of my body.

POINTS TO CONSIDER

? How might the producer stress the darkness inside Macbeth's castle?

? 35 What means does Lady Macbeth use here to shake Macbeth's resolve?

? 54–59 Which earlier lines do these recall? What impression of Lady Macbeth is conveyed here?

? 82–83 Which earlier images do these lines recall?

ACT ONE SCENE 7 SUGGESTED ACTIVITIES

Production/Group Work

P1 This scene contains an important struggle of wills between Macbeth and Lady Macbeth. In groups, discuss the means by which Lady Macbeth exerts control over her husband. Then, in pairs, re-enact the conversation that takes place between them, but as a 20th-century husband and wife arguing over a crucial decision that will affect their future life together.

Text

T1 Here is a three-part exercise designed to make you aware of Shakespeare's choice of words. Re-read lines 12–28 of Macbeth's soliloquy. Then, working in pairs and without the text, fill in the words missing from the speech below. (Write your words in a list on a separate sheet of paper, not in the book.) Try to use Shakespeare's original words if you can remember them. If not, use words that seem appropriate to you.
He's here in double _____ :

First, as I am his _____ and his _____,
Strong both against the deed; then, as his _____,
Who should against the murderer shut the _____,
Not _____ the knife myself. Besides, this Duncan
Hath borne his faculties so _____, hath been
So _____ in his great office, that his _____
Will plead like _____, trumpet-tongu'd, against
The deep damnation of his taking-off;
And _____, like a naked new-born babe,
Striding the blast, or heaven's _____ hors'd
Upon the sightless couriers of the air,
Shall blow the horrid deed in every eye,
That _____ shall drown the wind.

b) Look at the speech in the text and write down the original words in a list next to your own. Now, with your partner, compare the two lists of words. If you have used different words, discuss with your partner what effect Shakespeare's words convey and how they are different from yours. This may involve the meaning of the words. It may also involve rhythm or the way in which imagery is used. (See Shakespeare's Style p.145).

T2 Working alone, write down a list of all the arguments Macbeth uses against murdering Duncan.

T3 Add more images to your Image Trees.

Written Work

W1 Imagine that a lawyer or a barrister has been appointed to defend Macbeth. How do you think s/he might write her/his defence at this stage?

Act Two

SCENE 1

Inverness. The court of Macbeth's castle.
Banquo *enters followed by* **Fleance**, *with a torch before him.*

Banquo
How goes the night, boy?
Fleance
The moon is down; I have not heard the clock.
Banquo
And she goes down at twelve.
Fleance   I tak't, 'tis later, sir.
Banquo
Hold, take my sword. There's husbandry in heaven;
Their candles are all out. Take thee that too.   5
A heavy summons lies like lead upon me,
And yet I would not sleep. Merciful powers,
Restrain in me the cursed thoughts that nature
Gives way to in repose!

Enter **Macbeth** *and a* **Servant** *with a torch.*

Give me my sword.
Who's there?   10
Macbeth
A friend
Banquo
What, sir, not yet at rest? The king's a-bed.
He hath been in unusual pleasure, and

This scene takes place late at night, out of doors in the courtyard of Macbeth's castle. **What is the effect of this?**

1–4 Performances took place in the Elizabethan theatre in the afternoon between two and five when it was light. Hence the need to indicate night time in words.
4 *husbandry* economy, thrift. Through this image Shakespeare humorously conveys the idea of energy conservation in heaven since the candles (stars) are all snuffed out.

Sent forth great largess to your offices.
This diamond he greets your wife withal,
By the name of most kind hostess; and shut up
In measureless content.

Macbeth   Being unprepar'd,
Our will became the servant to defect,
Which else should free have wrought.

Banquo   All's well.
I dreamt last night of the three Weird Sisters.   20
To you they have show'd some truth.

Macbeth   I think not of them;
Yet, when we can entreat an hour to serve,
We would spend it in some words upon that business,
If you would grant the time.

Banquo   At your kind'st leisure.

Macbeth
If you shall cleave to my consent, when 'tis,   25
It shall make honour for you.

Banquo   So I lose none
In seeking to augment it, but still keep
My bosom franchis'd and allegiance clear,
I shall be counsell'd.

Macbeth   Good repose the while!

Banquo
Thanks, sir; the like to you!   30

                Banquo *and* **Fleance** *depart*

Macbeth
Go bid thy mistress, when my drink is ready,
She strike upon the bell. Get thee to bed.

                The **Servant** *goes.*

Is this a dagger which I see before me,
The handle toward my hand? Come, let me clutch thee:
I have thee not, and yet I see thee still.   35
Art thou not, fatal vision, sensible
To feeling as to sight? or art thou but
A dagger of the mind, a false creation,

14 *largess* gifts

16 *shut up* Duncan has retired to bed in a state of complete happiness.

17–19 Because we were unprepared, we could not be as hospitable as we wanted to be.

20 Why does Banquo introduce the subject of the witches?

22 *entreat....serve* when we can find a convenient hour.

25 *cleave to my consent, when 'tis* follow my advice when the time comes.

27 *My bosom franchis'd, and allegiance clear* as long as I can keep a clear conscience and not compromise my loyalty in any way. **What does the word 'allegiance' suggest about Banquo's feelings towards Macbeth?**

31 *bell* a prearranged signal from Lady Macbeth that all is ready.

31–64 Soliloquy. We know how much Macbeth has been witholding from Banquo. Now Shakespeare reveals his innermost thoughts and his final dilemma.

33 *dagger* **What is the significance of the dagger's handle pointing towards Macbeth's hand?**

36 *sensible....sight?* Macbeth asks whether the dagger can be touched as well as seen.

Proceeding from the heat-oppressed brain?
I see thee yet, in form as palpable 40
As this which now I draw.
Thou marshall'st me the way that I was going;
And such an instrument I was to use.
Mine eyes are made the fools o'th'other senses,
Or else worth all the rest: I see thee still; 45
And on thy blade and dudgeon gouts of blood,
Which was not so before. There's no such thing:
It is the bloody business which informs
Thus to mine eyes. Now o'er the one half-world
Nature seems dead, and wicked dreams abuse 50
The curtain'd sleep; witchcraft celebrates
Pale Hecate's offerings; and wither'd murder,
Alarum'd by his sentinel, the wolf,
Whose howl's his watch, thus with his stealthy pace,
With Tarquin's ravishing strides, towards his design 55
Moves like a ghost. Thou sure and firm-set earth,
Hear not my steps which way they walk, for fear
Thy very stones prate of my whereabout
And take the present horror from the time,
Which now suits with it. Whiles I threat, he lives: 60
Words to the heat of deeds too cold breath gives.

A bell rings.

I go, and it is done; the bell invites me.
Hear it not, Duncan, for it is a knell
That summons thee to heaven or to hell.

He goes.

39 *heat oppressed brain* feverish state of mind.
40 *palpable* touchable.
42 *marshall'st* directs – that is, pointing Macbeth in the direction of the sleeping Duncan.
44–45 Either I am seeing things or only my eyes can be trusted and the other senses are worth nothing.
46 *dudgeon* handle. *gouts* drops
48 *the bloody business* the idea of murder working on my imagination.
49 *half-world* where it is now night.
50–60 The world of night is the world of evil. Macbeth knows that he is about to enter that world.
51 *curtain'd* with closed eyelids or with curtains round the bed (a four-poster).
52 *Hecate* she was the goddess of witchcraft. She is imagined here performing her rites.
52 *wither'd Murder* murder is seen as a skeletal, threatening old man.
53 *sentinel* guard. The wolf is seen as being on duty doing a night watch for Murder.
54 *Whose howl's his watch* The wolf also acts as Murder's timekeeper, waking him up with his howl.
55 *Tarquin* murder is now seen as Tarquin. He was a Roman king who came at night to rape the virtuous Lucretia, his friend's wife.
58 *prate* talk, gossip.
59–60 *take…with it* break the horrifying silence and thus destroy the atmosphere appropriate to the terrible crime.
60 *threat* threaten.
61 Talking destroys the passion needed to act.
63 *knell* funeral bell.

POINTS TO CONSIDER

? Enter Banquo and Fleance. Why has Shakespeare introduced Banquo's son at this particular moment in the play?

? 6–9 Shakespeare here gives an important insight into Banquo's recent frame of mind. What is it?

? 21–23 This exchange is crucial for its insight into the characters of both Banquo and Macbeth. What do we learn of each?

ACT TWO SCENE 1 SUGGESTED ACTIVITIES

Production/Group Work

P1 Banquo and Macbeth are both hiding their innermost thoughts from each other during this exchange. In pairs, discuss how as producer and actor, you might make this clear to the audience.

P2 Imagine that you were producing this scene a) on stage, b) for television, c) as a film. Discuss in groups whether or not in each case you would use a real dagger for the soliloquy.

P3. There are a number of different ways of delivering Macbeth's soliloquy, eg terrified, bewildered, confident. In groups of three, each take on a different tone to deliver the speech and then discuss which is the most convincing.

Text

T1 a) Re-read Macbeth's soliloquy, lines 33–61. Then, working in pairs and without the text, fill in the words missing from the speech below. (Write your words in a list on a separate piece of paper, not in the book). Try to use Shakespeare's original words if you can remember them. If not, use words that seem appropriate to you.

Is this a _____ which I see before me,
The _____ toward my hand? Come let me _____ thee:
I have thee not, and yet I _____ thee still.
Art thou not, _____ vision, _____
To feeling as to _____ or art thou but
A dagger of the _____, a false creation,
Proceeding from the _____ _____ brain?
I see thee yet, in form as _____
As this which now I draw.
Thou _____ me the way that I was going;
And such an _____ I was to use.
Mine _____ are made the fools o'th'other senses,
Or else worth all the rest: I _____ thee still;
And on thy _____ and dudgeon _____ if blood,
Which was not so before. There's no such thing:
It is the _____ business which informs
Thus to mine eyes.

b) When you have finished, look at the speech in the text and write down the original words in a list next to your own. Now, with your partner, compare the two lists of words. If you have used different words, discuss with your partner what effect Shakespeare's words convey and how they are different from yours.

c) Now, working on your own and using Shakespeare's original words (from your second list), write down briefly what they suggest about Macbeth's state of mind.

T2 Add more images to your Image Trees.

W1 Write up Banquo's entry for his diary for that day giving some indication of his reaction to his conversation with Macbeth.

W2 We learn later on in the play (Three.4.line 62) that Lady Macbeth knows about Macbeth's vision of the dagger. This means that Macbeth must have told her at some stage. Write out how you imagine the conversation between them might have gone.

SCENE 2

Inverness. Macbeth's castle.
Enter **Lady Macbeth**

Lady Macbeth
    That which hath made them drunk hath made me bold;
    What hath quench'd them hath given me fire. Hark!
      Peace!
    It was the owl that shriek'd, the fatal bellman,
    Which gives the stern'st good-night. He is about it.
    The doors are open; and the surfeited grooms   5
    Do mock their charge with snores. I have drugg'd their possets,
    That death and nature do contend about them,
    Whether they live or die.
Macbeth(*within*)   Who's there! What, ho!
Lady Macbeth
    Alack! I am afraid they have awak'd,
    And 'tis not done; th'attempt, and not the deed,   10
    Confounds us. Hark! I laid their daggers ready;

This scene is a continuation of the previous one and therefore the setting is identical. The audience will, however, be aware that nearby is the guest chamber of the sleeping Duncan.

1 *bold* Lady Macbeth has been drinking too! **What does this suggest about her own state of mind?**

2 *quench'd them* She compares the sleepy effect of alcohol upon the bodyguards to water extinguishing a fire. In contrast, she points out that the alcohol has set her alight and given her courage.

2 *Hark! Peace!* **What is the effect of these words?**

3 *fatal bellman* the man whose job it was to ring a funeral bell outside the door of a condemned prisoner.

4 *stern'st goodnight* the final and therefore the most solemn farewell the condemned man receives.

4 *He is about it* **What does this indicate about Lady Macbeth's state of mind?**

5 *surfeited grooms* Duncan's drunken attendants.

6 *mock their charge with snores* The snoring of the bodyguards goes to show just how much they have failed in their duty to protect the King.

6 *possets* a hot drink taken at nights, usually containing alcohol as well as milk and spices.

7–8 *death . . . die* Life and Death are seen as two men fighting to decide whether the bodyguards should live or die.

11 *confounds* ruins. Lady Macbeth fears that if Macbeth has failed, they will be caught out and condemned even before committing the murder.

He could not miss 'em. Had he not resembled
My father as he slept, I had done't.

Enter Macbeth

My husband!

Macbeth
I have done the deed. Didst thou not hear a noise?

Lady Macbeth
I heard the owl scream and the crickets cry.   15
Did not you speak?

Macbeth   When?

Lady Macbeth   Now.

Macbeth   As I descended?

Lady Macbeth
Ay.

Macbeth
Hark!
Who lies i'th second chamber?

Lady Macbeth   Donalbain.

Macbeth (*looking at his hands*)
This is a sorry sight.   20

Lady Macbeth
A foolish thought to say a sorry sight.

Macbeth
There's one did laugh in's sleep, and one cried 'Murder!'
That they did wake each other. I stood and heard them;
But they did say their prayers, and address'd them
Again to sleep.

Lady Macbeth   There are two lodg'd together.   25

Macbeth
One cried 'God bless us,' and 'Amen' the other,
As they had seen me with these hangman's hands.
List'ning their fear, I could not say 'Amen',
When they did say 'God bless us!'

Lady Macbeth
Consider it not so deeply.   30

Macbeth
But wherefore could I not pronounce 'Amen'?

12–13 *Had he . . . done't* **What do these lines suggest about Lady Macbeth?**

13 *My husband* **What is the effect of these words?**

15 *owl, cricket* both heralds of death, according to Elizabethan belief.

15–21 Notice the irregularity of these lines. **What does Shakespeare convey here in terms of atmosphere?**

19 *second chamber* The guestchamber of large stately homes usually had another chamber next to it, here occupied by Malcolm and Donalbain. Strangely, Lady Macbeth only mentions Donalbain by name. **Could there be a reason for this?**

20 *sorry* sad, miserable.

21 *they, them* Malcolm and Donalbain.

25 *lodg'd* sharing the same room.

27 *As* as if. *hangman's hands* usually covered in blood because hanging also involved 'drawing'(the entrails from the body), and 'quartering' (the body into pieces).

I had most need of blessing, and 'Amen'
Stuck in my throat.

Lady Macbeth   These deeds must not be thought
After these ways: so, it will make us mad.

Macbeth
    Methought I heard a voice cry, 'Sleep no more!   35
    Macbeth does murder sleep' the innocent sleep,
    Sleep that knits up the ravell'd sleave of care,
    The death of each day's life, sore labour's bath,
    Balm of hurt minds, great nature's second course,
    Chief nourisher in life's feast.

Lady Macbeth   What do you mean?   40

Macbeth
    Still it cried, 'Sleep no more' to all the house,
    'Glamis hath murder'd sleep; and therefore Cawdor
    Shall sleep no more, Macbeth shall sleep no more.'

Lady Macbeth
    Who was it that thus cried? Why, worthy Thane,
    You do unbend your noble strength to think   45
    So brainsickly of things. Go, get some water
    And wash this filthy witness from your hand.
    Why did you bring these daggers from the place?
    They must lie there. Go carry them, and smear
    The sleepy grooms with blood.

Macbeth   I'll go no more: 50
    I am afraid to think what I have done;
    Look on't again I dare not.

Lady Macbeth   Infirm of purpose!
    Give me the daggers. The sleeping and the dead
    Are but as pictures; 'tis the eye of childhood
    That fears a painted devil. If he do bleed,   55
    I'll gild the faces of the grooms withal,
    For it must seem their guilt.

She goes. Knocking within.

Macbeth   Whence is that knocking?
How is't with me, when every noise appals me?
What hands are here? Ha! They pluck out mine eyes.

33–34 *These deeds . . . mad* important lines to remember in view of what happens later in the play.

37 *knits up . . . care* sleep smooths out our troubles, just as tangled wool or silk (ravell'd sleave) is first untangled before use.

38 *sore labour's bath* sleep has a similar effect to a hot bath after a hard day's work.

39 *Balm* soothing oil or ointment.

39–40 *great nature's . . . feast* the first course of a feast was usually only small while the main meat dish came second.
Macbeth points out in this speech how fundamental sleep is to the health of both body and mind.

45 *unbend* reduce, weaken like someone unstringing a bow.

47 *filthy witness* the blood that would provide evidence against him.

48 Why has Lady Macbeth only just noticed the daggers? What is the effect of the discovery upon her?

53–55 *The sleeping . . . devil* **These words contradict earlier ones in the same scene. Which ones?**

55 *a painted devil* a picture of a devil.

56 *gild* to coat, usually with a precious metal (gilt), but here by spreading a thin layer of blood over them. Lady Macbeth is punning (see Glossary) on the word 'guilt' to heighten the tension of the occasion.

59 *pluck out mine eyes* Macbeth feels as if his own eyes are almost being pulled out of their sockets by the sight of the blood on his hands.

Will all great Neptune's ocean wash this blood   60
Clean from my hand? No, this my hand will rather
The multitudinous seas incarnadine,
Making the green one red.

Re enter **Lady Macbeth**

Lady Macbeth
My hands are of your colour; but I shame
To wear a heart so white. (*Knock*) I hear a knocking   65
At the south entry; retire we to our chamber.
A little water clears us of this deed.
How easy is it then! Your constancy
Hath left you unattended. (*Knock*) Hark! more knocking.
Get on your nightgown, lest occasion call us   70
And show us to be watchers. Be not lost
So poorly in your thoughts.
Macbeth
To know my deed, 'twere best not know myself. (*Knock*)
Wake Duncan with thy knocking! I would thou couldst!

They go

60 *Neptune* the Roman god of the sea.
62 *multitudinous* vast amounts. *incarnadine* turn scarlet red.
63 turning the green sea red all over.
65 *white* here used in the sense of cowardly.
67 *a little . . . deed* again these lines should be noted and contrasted with what happens in the final act.
68 *Your constancy . . . unattended* your courage has left you.
70–71 *lest occasion . . . watchers* in case they call for us and find us still awake.
72 *poorly* weakly, feebly.
73 *To know . . . myself* in reply to Lady Macbeth, Macbeth suggests that it might be better not to know himself than to face up to the knowledge of the crime he has committed.

Points to Consider

? 15–21 What insight are we given into the state of mind of Macbeth and Lady Macbeth during this exchange?

? 35–40 What aspect of Duncan's murder has most upset Macbeth?

? 44 *Who . . . hand* What does Lady Macbeth reveal of herself here? What modern expression might she have used here in talking to Macbeth?

? 52 *Infirm of purpose!* What method does Lady Macbeth employ to persuade Macbeth to act? Where else have we seen her behave in this way?

? 57 *Whence is that knocking?* In Macbeth's present state of mind, where might he feel the knocking is coming from?

ACT TWO SCENE 2 SUGGESTED ACTIVITIES

Production/Group Work

P1 Obtain a photocopy each of the scene. Working in threes, either write directly on to your paper or stick it onto a larger sheet to give you more writing space. Then go through the scene together as if you were producing the play, writing notes in the margins. These notes can refer to any aspect of the scene in production, but pay particular attention to the way Macbeth and Lady Macbeth behave, the way they speak and how they actually reveal their feelings to the audience.

P2 Much of this scene is about guilt and its effect on people's behaviour. In pairs, act out a modern version of the scene. The crime can be of any nature, but the emphasis of your scene should be on your reactions to that crime.

P3 Working in groups of four, take on the roles of Macbeth, Lady Macbeth and two interviewers. Carry out the interviews one after the other to find out how each character has reacted to the murder.

Text

T1 Reread Macbeth's speech, lines 35-39. Then, working in pairs and without the text, fill in the words missing from the speech below. (Write your words on a separate piece of paper, not in the book.) Try to use Shakespeare's original words if you can remember them. If not, use words that seem appropriate to you.

Methought I heard a voice cry, '_____ no more!
Macbeth does murder sleep' the _____ sleep,
Sleep that knits up the ravell'd sleave of _____,
The death of each day's life, sore labour's _____,
_____ of hurt minds, great nature's second course,
Chief _____ in life's feast.

b) When you have finished, look at the speech in the text and write down the original words in a list next to your own. Now, with your partner, compare the two lists of words. If you have used different words, discuss with your partner what effect Shakespeare's words convey and how they are different from yours.

c) Working alone and using Shakespeare's original words (from your second list), write down briefly what Shakespeare is saying about sleep.

T2 Add more images to your Image Trees.

Written Work

W1 Imagine you witness the murder of Duncan. Describe what you see.

W2 Make a list of all the things in this scene which are not what they seem.

W3 Lady Macbeth is now emerging with some odd contrasts in her character. In two columns, list some of these contrasts.

SCENE 3

Inverness. Macbeth's castle.
Knocking from within. Enter a **Porter**

Porter

Here's a knocking indeed! If a man were porter of
hell-gate, he should have old turning the key. (*Knocking*)
Knock, knock, knock! Who's there, i'the name of
Beelzebub? Here's a farmer that hang'd himself on
th'expectation of plenty. Come in timeserver, have   5
napkins enow about you; here you'll sweat for't.
(*Knocking*) Knock, knock! Who's there, i'th'other devil's
name? Faith, here's an equivocator, that could swear in
both the scales against either scale; who committed
treason enough for God's sake, yet could not   10
equivocate to heaven. O, come in, equivocator.
(*Knocking*) Knock, knock! Who's there? Faith, here's an
English tailor come hither for stealing out of a French
hose: come in, tailor, here you may roast your goose.
(*Knocking*) Knock, knock; never at quiet! What are you?   15
But this place is too cold for hell. I'll devil-porter
it no further. I had thought to have let in some of all
professions that go the primrose way to th'everlasting
bonfire. (*Knocking*) Anon, Anon! (*Opening the gate*) I pray
you remember the porter.   20

Enter **Macduff** *and* **Lennox**

Macduff

Was it so late, friend, ere you went to bed, that you
do lie so late?

Porter

Faith, sir, we were carousing till the second cock; and
drink, sir, is a great provoker of three things.

Macduff

What three things does drink especially provoke?   25

Porter

Marry, sir, nose-painting, sleep, and urine. Lechery,

The setting is identical to the last scene but the Porter enters in a drunken state. **What will be the effect of his appearance on the audience?**

2 *old* plenty of, frequent.

4 *Beelzebub* a devil, the second in command to Satan. The Porter imagines Macbeth's castle to be Hell and he himself the keeper of the gates of Hell. He describes a number of the damned waiting to be let in through the gates.

4–5 *Here's a farmer . . . plenty* A farmer who had hoarded corn in the hope of a good profit might well commit suicide if, following a good harvest, the price of corn had fallen.

5 *Come in timeserver* he beckons the farmer into Hell, reminding him that he had become a slave to time.

6 *napkins* handkerchiefs, to wipe away sweat.

7 *other devil* he's forgotten his name.

8 *equivocator* a person who uses words to conceal the truth, who does not actually lie, but who doesn't tell the truth either.(See earlier chapter 'Killing a King' **Who has already *equivocated* in the play?**

8–9 *swear . . . scale* whose contradictions balanced each other out. Justice is seen here as a woman holding scales to show that both sides are given a fair and equal hearing.

10–11 *could not . . . heaven* This seems to be a reference to a Jesuit priest called Henry Garnet, who had been tried in 1606 for defending the conspirators in the Gunpowder Plot. He used equivocation as a means of defence.

13–14 *stealing . . . hose* the tailor has been caught stealing material when making breeches. Because these were tight (French style), he was caught out.

14 *goose* this refers to the smoothing iron used by a tailor.

16 *devil-porter* be the porter at the gates of Hell.

18–19 *primrose way . . . bonfire* the easy and attractive route to Hell.

19 *Anon* I'm coming.

20 *remember the porter* he is asking for a tip!

23 *carousing* drinking heavily. *second cock* 3.0 a.m.

26 *Marry* by Mary. *nose-painting* heavy drinking gives you a red nose.

sir, it provokes and unprovokes: it provokes the desire,
but it takes away the performance. Therefore, much drink
may be said to be an equivocator with lechery: it makes
him, and it mars him; it sets him on, and it takes   30
him off; it persuades him, and disheartens him; makes
him stand to, and not stand to; in conclusion,
equivocates him in a sleep, and, giving him the lie,
leaves him.

Macduff
I believe drink gave thee the lie last night.   35

Porter
That it did, sir, i'the very throat on me; but I requited
him for his lie; and, I think, being too strong for him,
though he took up my legs sometime, yet I made a shift
to cast him.

Macduff
Is thy master stirring?   40

Enter Macbeth

Our knocking has awak'd him; here he comes.

Lennox
Good morrow, noble sir.

Macbeth   Good morrow, both.

Macduff
Is the King stirring, worthy Thane?

Macbeth   Not yet.

Macduff
He did command me to call timely on him;
I have almost slipp'd the hour.

Macbeth   I'll bring you to him.   45

Macduff
I know this is a joyful trouble to you;
But yet 'tis one.

Macbeth
The labour we delight in physics pain.
This is the door.

Macduff   I'll make so bold to call,
For 'tis my limited service.   50

26–32 *Lechery . . . lust* the Porter describes with some relish the way that drink arouses the sexual appetite of the drinker but then also renders him impotent. He repeats the idea several times.

32–34 *in conclusion . . . him* the Porter finally suggests that drink cheats a man in his sleep by giving him passionate dreams but then leaving him with the dreams unfulfilled.

35 *gave thee the lie* a play on the word *lie* meaning *laid you out* as in boxing or wrestling.

36 *i'the very throat on me* directly.

38 *he took up my legs sometime* drink made me fall over.

38–39 *yet I . . . him* I tried to throw him down (again as in wrestling) by urinating.

44 *timely* early.

45 *slipp'd the hour* missed the time.

46 *joyful trouble* a pleasurable duty.

48 *physics* cures.

50 *limited service* what I have been instructed to do.

Macduff *goes*

Lennox

Goes the King hence today?

Macbeth

He does; he did appoint so.

Lennox

The night has been unruly. Where we lay,
Our chimneys were blown down; and, as thy say,
Lamentings heard i'th'air; strange screams of death,   55
And prophesying, with accents terrible
Of dire combustion and confus'd events
New hatch'd to th' woeful time; the obscure bird
Clamour'd the livelong night. Some say the earth
Was feverous and did shake.

Macbeth   'Twas a rough night.   60

Lennox

My young remembrance cannot parallel
A fellow to it.

Re-enter **Macduff**

Macduff

O horror! horror! horror! Tongue nor heart
Cannot conceive nor name thee!

Macbeth and Lennox   What's the matter?

Macduff

Confusion now hath made his masterpiece!   65
Most sacrilegious murder hath broke ope
The Lord's anointed temple, and stole thence
The life o'the building.

Macbeth   What is't you say? the life?

Lennox

Mean you his Majesty?

Macduff

Approach the chamber, and destroy your sight   70
With a new Gorgon. Do not bid me speak;
See, and then speak yourselves.

Macbeth and Lennox *go*

57–58 *of dire . . . time* Lennox is describing the chaos and confusion which he sees as a direct result of the war with Norway (*woeful time*). What else could it refer to?

58 *obscure bird* the owl, obscure because it is a night bird and therefore lives in darkness.

61–62 *My young . . . it* I can't remember a night like it in my life.

65–68 *Confusion. . . . building* Macduff's words reflect the Elizabethan belief in the Divine Right of Kings (See 'Killing a King' p11). The attack on the King is seen not only as an attack upon God, but also upon the ordered state of the country.

66 *sacrilegious* unholy, profane.

67 *The Lord's anointed temple* Duncan would have been anointed with holy oil when he was crowned. Duncan's body here is seen as a holy temple which has been broken open.

71 *Gorgon* a monster called Medusa in Greek mythology. She and her two sisters had snakes for hair and turned to stone all who looked on them. Macduff suggests that the sight of Duncan's body will do the same to them.

Awake! awake!
Ring the alarum bell. Murder and treason!
Banquo and Donalbain! Malcolm! awake!
Shake off this downy sleep, death's counterfeit,   75
And look on death itself. Up, up, and see
The great doom's image! Malcolm! Banquo!
As from your graves rise up and walk like sprites
To countenancee this horror! Ring the bell.

The bell rings. Enter **Lady Macbeth**

Lady Macbeth
  What's the business,   80
That such a hideous trumpet calls to parley
The sleepers of the house? Speak, speak!

Macduff
  O gentle lady,
'Tis not for you to hear what I can speak:
The repetition in a woman's ear
Would murder as it fell.

Enter **Banquo**

    O Banquo! Banquo!
Our royal master's murder'd!

Lady Macbeth   Woe, alas!
What! in our house?

Banquo   Too cruel anywhere.
Dear Duff, I prithee, contradict thyself,
And say it is not so.   90

Re-enter **Macbeth and Lennox**

Macbeth
Had I but died an hour before this chance,
I had liv'd a blessed time; for, from this instant,
There's nothing serious in mortality;
All is but toys; renown and grace is dead;
The wine of life is drawn, and the mere lees   95
Is left this vault to brag of.

Enter **Malcolm and Donalbain**

---

75 *downy sleep, death's counterfeit* gentle sleep, and therefore only an imitation of death, not the real thing.

77 *The great doom's image!* a sight which will be as dreadful as the Day of Judgement.

78 *sprites* ghosts or spirits.

79 *countenance* face.

Enter Lady Macbeth **What expression will she have on her face?**

81 *hideous* harsh, strident. She compares it to a trumpet sounded at battle, calling the men to a truce (*parley*).

85–86 To repeat what has happened here in a woman's ear would kill her.

89 *What! in our house?* **What appears to be Lady Macbeth's main concern?**

91 *this chance* this happening.

93 *serious in mortality* nothing important left in life.

94 *toys* of no value, trifles.

95 *The wine . . . brag of* Macbeth sees the world as a wine cellar from which all the good wine has been drawn and only the dregs (*lees*) are left.

Donalbain
    What's amiss?
Macbeth   You are, and do not know't.
    The spring, the head, the fountain of your blood,
    Is stopp'd; the very source of it is stopp'd.
Macduff
    Your royal father's murder'd.
Malcolm   O! by whom?   100
Lennox
    Those of his chamber, as it seem'd, had done't.
    Their hands and faces were all badg'd with blood;
    So were their daggers, which unwip'd we found
    Upon their pillows. They star'd and were distracted;
    No man's life was to be trusted with them.   105
Macbeth
    O, yet I do repent me of my fury
    That I did kill them.
Macduff   Wherefore did you so?
Macbeth
    Who can be wise, amaz'd, temp'rate, and furious,
    Loyal and neutral, in a moment? No man.
    The expedition of my violent love   110
    Outrun the pauser reason. Here lay Duncan,
    His silver skin lac'd with his golden blood;
    And his gash'd stabs look'd like a breach in nature
    For ruin's wasteful entrance: there, the murderers,
    Steep'd in the colours of their trade, their daggers 115
    Unmannerly breech'd with gore. Who could refrain,
    That had a heart to love, and in that heart
    Courage to make's love known?
Lady Macbeth   Help me hence, ho!
Macduff
    Look to the lady.
Malcolm (*aside to* **Donalbain**)
    Why do we hold our tongues that most may claim   120
    This argument for ours?
Donalbain (*aside to* **Malcolm**) What should be spoken
    Here, where our fate, hid in an auger-hole,

97 *You are . . . know't* Macbeth refers back to *amiss* to describe Malcolm and Donalbain's state that is, ruined.

98 *The spring . . . stopp'd* these all refer to the source from which water springs and, in the case of Donalbain and Malcolm, their father.

102 *badg'd* splashed or marked.

106 *O yet . . . them* the audience only learns this news now at the same time as Macduff. **How does Macduff react? How do you react?**

108 *temp'rate* controlled, restrained.

110 *expedition* haste, speed.

111 *pauser reason* reason which makes us stop in our tracks and think again.

113–114 *his gash'd stabs . . . entrance* Macbeth compares Duncan's wounds to breaches or breaks in a city's walls through which an enemy could force an entry and destroy the city.

115 *steep'd* dyed.

116 *Unmannerly . . . gore* using a clothing image, Macbeth suggests that the daggers of the grooms are indecently covered up to the hilt with blood like a pair of trousers.

116 *refrain* stop himself.

118 *Help me hence, ho!* Lady Macbeth announces that she is going to faint! **What is really happening here?**

120–121 Malcolm wonders why he and Donalbain are keeping quiet since they have most reason to grieve.

What contrast is Shakespeare making?

122 *auger hole* An auger is a carpenter's tool used for piercing holes in wood. Donalbain realises that danger may be lying in wait for them in the smallest, most unlikely place. **How else is an auger hole appropiate here?**

May rush and seize us? Let's away:
Our tears are not yet brew'd.

Malcolm (*aside to* **Donalbain**) Nor our strong sorrow
Upon the foot of motion.

Banquo   Look to the lady.   125

Lady Macbeth is carried out

And when we have our naked frailties hid,
That suffer in exposure, let us meet,
And question this most bloody piece of work,
To know it further. Fears and scruples shake us.
In the great hand of God I stand, and thence   130
Against the undivulg'd pretence I fight
Of treasonous malice.

Macduff   And so do I.

All   So all.

Macbeth
Let's briefly put on manly readiness
And meet i'the hall together.

All   Well contented.

All but **Malcolm and Donalbain** *go out*

Malcolm
What will you do? Let's not consort with them: 135
To show an unfelt sorrow is an office
Which the false man does easy. I'll to England.

Donalbain
To Ireland I; our separated fortune
Shall keep us both the safer: where we are,
There's daggers in men's smiles: the near in blood,   140
The nearer blood.

Malcolm   This murderous shaft that's shot
Hath not yet lighted, and our safest way
Is to avoid the aim. Therefore to horse;
And let us not be dainty of leave-taking,
But shift away. There's warrant in that theft   145
Which steals itself, when there's no mercy left.

They go

124 *our tears . . . brew'd* we're not yet ready to cry. **What is implied here about Macbeth?**

125 *Upon the foot of motion* ready to be shown.

126–127 *And when . . . exposure* Banquo sees their bodies clad only in night clothes as weak and exposed. **Could he be referring to anything else?**

129 *scruples* doubts and uncertainties.

131 *undivulg'd pretence* secret plan.

132 *treasonous malice* the hatred that has killed a king.

133 *manly readiness* men's clothes, **but, bearing in mind lines 126–127, what else could he be referring to?**

135 *consort* mix.

136 *office* duty.

138–139 *our separated . . . safer* it will be safer for us to go our separate ways. **How is this true?**

140 *daggers in men's smiles* **what does this mean?**

140–141 *the near . . . nearer bloody* the more closely we are related to the King, the more we are in danger.

141 *shaft* arrow.

142 *lighted* reached its target.

143 *avoid the aim* keep away from the hand of the archer. **Who is the archer?**

144 *dainty* fussy.

145 *shift away* steal away.

145–146 *There's warrant . . . left* we are quite justified in leaving so discourteously when our host is such a ruthless man.

POINTS TO CONSIDER

? Why do you think Shakespeare has introduced a drunken Porter into the play at this moment?

? 4 In what ways is Macbeth's castle like Hell?

? 26–32 How would the Elizabethan audience react to this speech? See 'An Afternoon at the Globe Theatre' (p 4).

? 81 How is the battle image appropriate here?

? 85–86 How do you react to these words being used about Lady Macbeth?

? 89 What does this line really reveal about Lady Macbeth?

? 91–96 What do you notice about the way Macbeth speaks? Is he giving away any of his inner feelings?

? 113–114 Who else has made use of a battle image in this scene? What could a close observer learn from this?

? 116 What does the language of this line suggest about Macbeth's state of mind?

? 130–133 What do these three lines tell us of Banquo's character?

? 136–137 What important information is the audience given here?

? 143 Malcolm and Donalbain have expressed the same idea in three different ways. What are they really saying and why are they saying it indirectly?

ACT TWO SCENE 3 SUGGESTED ACTIVITIES

Production/Group Work

P1 Obtain a photocopy of lines 80–125 (Lady Macbeth's appearance). In pairs, write in detailed stage directions and production notes for actors taking part in the play.
Pay particular attention to the way Macbeth and Lady Macbeth behave, the way they speak and how they actually reveal their feelings to the audience.

P2 A group of eight should take on roles for each of the following: Lady Macbeth, Macbeth, Porter, Macduff, Banquo, Malcolm, Donalbain and a Detective. The rest of the class should act as a jury. Assume the Detective has arrived at the scene of the crime just as Malcolm and Donalbain are about to leave. S/he should interview each of the above suspects in turn in front of the class, but not in front of any of the other suspects. At the end a decision should be taken on who committed the murder a) by the Detective and b) by the class. Base your decision only on the evidence given during the interviews, not on the play.

Test

T1 Add more images to your Image Trees.

T2a) Re-read Macbeth's speech, lines 108–118. Then, working in pairs and without the text, fill in the words missing from the speech below. (Write your words in a list on a separate sheet of paper, not in the book.) Try to use Shakespeare's original words if you can remember them. If not, use words that seem appropriate to you.
Here lay Duncan,
His _____ skin lac'd with his _____ blood;
And his _____ stabs look'd like a breach in nature
For ruins _____ entrance: there, the murderers,
_____ in the colours of their trade, their daggers
Unmannerly breech'd with _____.

b) When you have finished, look at the speech in the text and write down the original words in a list next to your own. With you partner, compare the two lists of words. If you have used different words, discuss with your partner what effect Shakespeare's words convey and how they are different from yours. Discuss also what insight Shakespeare's words give into Macbeth's state of mind.

Written Work

W1 The Porter's words are not very clear to a modern audience without a great deal of explanation. Rewrite the Porter's speech for a 20th century audience, making it as humorous as you can.

W2 Malcolm and Donalbain are restricted in what they can say. Write out the conversation they might have once they have left Macbeth's castle and before they go their separate ways.

SCENE 4

Inverness. Outside Macbeth's castle.
Enter **Ross** *with an* **Old Man**

Old Man
    Threescore and ten I can remember well;
    Within the volume of which time I have seen
    Hours dreadful and things strange; but this sore night
    Hath trifled former knowings.

Setting the action now moves to outside Macbeth's castle. **What effect does this have upon the audience?**

1 *Threescore and ten* **what is the purpose of this detail?**
3–4 *but this sore . . . knowings* this dreadful night has made all that I can remember seem trivial by comparison.

Ross   Ah, good father,
 Thou seest the heavens, as troubled with man's act   5
 Threatens his bloody stage. By th'clock 'tis day,
 And yet dark night strangles the travelling lamp.
 Is't night's predominance, or the day's shame,
 That darkness does the face of earth entomb,
 When living light should kiss it?
Old Man   'Tis unnatural,   10
 Even like the deed that's done. On Tuesday last,
 A falcon, towering in her pride of place,
 Was by a mousing owl hawk'd at and kill'd.
Ross
 And Duncan's horses – a thing most strange and certain –
 Beauteous and swift, the minions of their race,   15
 Turn'd wild in nature, broke their stalls, flung out,
 Contending 'gainst obedience, as they would make
 War with mankind.
Old Man   'Tis said they ate each other.
Ross
 They did so, to the amazement of mine eyes,
 That look'd upon't.

                        Enter **Macduff**

                        Here comes the good Macduff.   20
 How goes the world, sir, now?
Macduff   Why, see you not?
Ross
 Is't known who did this more than bloody deed?
Macduff
 Those that Macbeth hath slain.
Ross   Alas, the day!
 What good could they pretend?
Macduff   They were suborn'd.
 Malcolm and Donalbain, the King's two sons,   25
 Are stol'n away and fled, which puts upon them
 Suspicion of the deed.
Ross   'Gainst nature still.
 Thriftless ambition, that wilt ravin up
 Thine own life's means! Then 'tis most like

5 *as* as though.
5–6 *heavens . . . stage* Ross suggests that the heavens have responded to the violent deeds on earth by threatening violence of their own, that is, bad weather. The earth is compared to a stage, the heavens the roof over it. (See the illustration of the Globe Theatre).
7 *strangles . . . lamp* obscures the sun with dark clouds.
8 *predominance* superiority.
9 *entomb* bury.
12–13 *A falcon . . . kill'd* a falcon is a bird of prey, so this is the opposite of what one might expect.
15 *minions of their race* the best and therefore the favourite of their kind.
16 *broke* broke out.
17 *contending . . . obedience* fighting against their training.
24 *what . . . pretend* what did they think they could get out of it?
24 *suborn'd* bribed to do the deed.
28–29 *Thriftless . . . means* Ross suggests that in destroying their own father and therefore their own life source, Malcolm and Donalbain's excessive ambition has gained nothing.

The sovereignty will fall upon Macbeth.   30
Macduff
    He is already nam'd, and gone to Scone
    To be invested.
Ross   Where is Duncan's body?
Macduff
    Carried to Colmekill,
    The sacred storehouse of his predecessors
    And guardian of their bones.
Ross   Will you to Scone?   35
Macduff
    No, cousin, I'll to Fife.
Ross   Well, I will thither.
Macduff
    Well, may you see things well done there: adieu,
    Lest our old robes sit easier than our new!
Ross
    Farewell, father.
Old Man
    God's benison go with you, and with those   40
    That would make good of bad, and friends of foes!

                They go

31 *nam'd* elected, the means by which a king was appointed in Scotland.
31 *Scone* Scottish kings were crowned here on the Stone of Destiny. This Stone was transferred to Westminister Abbey by Edward I in 1296. It is now in the coronation chair used by all British sovereigns.
32 *To be invested* to be made king through a coronation ceremony.
33 *Colmekill* a place in Iona where all Scottish kings were buried.
34 *Fife* Macduff's own home.
34 *thither* Ross is going to Scone for the coronation of Macbeth.
35–36 *Well . . . new* **What does Macduff mean here? What tone of voice is he likely to use in speaking these words?**
40 *benison* blessing.

POINTS TO CONSIDER

? The three references in this scene to the disturbances in nature all suggest the reversal of what would normally happen. Where else have we seen the reversal of the normal or the natural? What is Shakespeare suggesting

ACT TWO SCENE 4 SUGGESTED ACTIVITIES

Production/Group Work

P1 In pairs, discuss the importance of the Old Man in this scene. Why has Shakespeare introduced this new character at this stage? If, as producer of the play, you were short of actors, who could you use to double up to play the part of the Old Man?

P2 Still in pairs, look at the part played by Ross here and in Act One scene 2. Is his role in the two scenes in any way similar? What impression are you beginning to form of his character?

P3 Working in fours, imagine that you are producing this scene and discuss what atmosphere you will try to convey and how you would convey it.

Text

T1 Add more images to your Image Trees.

T2 List the unnatural events mentioned in this scene. Can you add any modern equivalent signs of bad luck?

Written Work

W1 Macduff has deliberately chosen not to go to Macbeth's coronation. He also seems to have a clear view of the recent state of affairs. Imagine he has now arrived home in Fife. Write out the conversation that he has with his wife.

Act Three

SCENE 1

Forres. A room in the palace.
Enter **Banquo**

Banquo
Thou hast it now, King, Cawdor, Glamis, all,
As the weird women promis'd; and, I fear,
Thou play'dst most foully for't; yet it was said
It should not stand in thy posterity;
But that myself should be the root and father   5
Of many kings. If there come truth from them
As upon thee, Macbeth, their speeches shine
Why, by the verities on thee made good,
May they not be my oracles as well
And set me up in hope? But. hush, no more.   10

Sennet sounded. Enter **Macbeth** *as King,* **Lady Macbeth** *as Queen;*
Lennox, Ross, Lords, Ladies *and* **Attendants.**

Macbeth
Here's our chief guest.
Lady Macbeth   If he had been forgotten,
It had been as a gap in our great feast,
And all-thing unbecoming.
Macbeth
Tonight we hold a solemn supper, sir,
And I'll request your presence.
Banquo   Let your Highness   15
Command upon me; to the which my duties

Duncan's palace at Forres is now, of course, inhabited by Macbeth.

4 *It...posterity* that the crown would not be inherited by your descendants.
6 *them* the witches.
7 *speeches shine* their words seem to cast favour, like the sun.
8 *verities...good* the words that have come true for you.
9 *oracles* prophets.
Sennet notes on the trumpet to indicate the arrival of someone of importance.
Enter Macbeth as King, Lady Macbeth as Queen **How will they look different from when we last saw them?**
14 *solemn supper* a formal banquet.
16 *to the which...knit* Banquo suggests that a command from the King is one that cannot be disobeyed. He uses the image of a knot that can never be undone. **What tone do you think he uses here? What might he really be thinking?**

Are with a most indissoluble tie
For ever knit.

Macbeth
Ride you this afternoon?

Banquo   Ay, my good lord.

Macbeth
We should have else desir'd your good advice –   20
Which still hath been both grave and prosperous –
In this day's council; but we'll take tomorrow.
Is't far you ride?

Banquo
As far, my lord, as will fill up the time
'Twixt this and supper. Go not my horse the better,   25
I must become a borrower of the night
For a dark hour or twain.

Macbeth   Fail not our feast.

Banquo
My lord, I will not.

Macbeth
We hear our bloody cousins are bestow'd
In England and in Ireland, not confessing   30
Their cruel parricide, filling their hearers
With strange invention; but of that tomorrow,
When, therewithal, we shall have cause of state
Craving us jointly. Hie you to horse; adieu,
Till you return at night. Goes Fleance with you?   35

Banquo
Ay, my good lord: our time does call upon's.

Macbeth
I wish your horses swift and sure of foot;
And so I do commend you to their backs.
Farewell. (**Banquo** *goes*)
Let every man be master of his time   40
Till seven at night; to make society
The sweeter welcome, we will keep ourself
Till supper-time alone; while then, God be with you!

All leave apart from **Macbeth** *and a* **Servant**

Sirrah, a word with you. Attend those men our pleasure?

19 *Ride...afternoon* the real reason for this question becomes clear a little later.

21 *still...prosperous* thoughtful and of great value to me.

22 *take* hear it.

25–27 *Go not...twain* Banquo suggests that he won't be back for an hour or two unless his horse goes faster than usual.

28 *bloody* because they murdered Duncan.

29 *bestow'd* settled down.

31 *parricide* the murder of their father.

32 *strange invention* suggesting that Macbeth himself might have been the murderer.

What have Malcolm and Donalbain been trying to do? How is Macbeth retaliating?

32–34 *but of that...jointly* but we'll say more of this tomorrow when, besides this, we shall discuss other state affairs which require the attention of us both.

34 *Hie you* hurry.

35 *Goes Fleance with you?* see notes line 19. **Who is Fleance? Can you see any reason for Macbeth's question?**

36 *our time...upon's* it's time we were going.

40 *master of his time* free to do as he wishes.

41 *to make society...alone* in order to appreciate the company even more tonight, I'll stay alone until supper.

43 *while* until.

44 *Attend* await.

Servant

    They are, my lord, without the palace gate.   45

Macbeth

    Bring them before us. (*The* **Servant** *goes*)

               To be thus is nothing,

    But to be safely thus. Our fears in Banquo

    Stick deep, and in his royalty of nature

    Reigns that which would be fear'd. 'Tis much he dares,

    And to that dauntless temper of his mind   50

    He hath a wisdom that doth guide his valour

    To act in safety. There is none but he

    Whose being I do fear; and under him

    My genius is rebuk'd, as it is said

    Mark Anthony's was by Caesar. He chid the Sisters   55

    When first they put the name of King upon me,

    And bade them speak to him; then, prophet-like,

    They hail'd him father to a line of kings.

    Upon my head they plac'd a fruitless crown

    And put a barren sceptre in my gripe,   60

    Thence to be wrench'd with an unlineal hand,

    No son of mine succeeding. If't be so,

    For Banquo's issue have I fil'd my mind;

    For them the gracious Duncan have I murder'd;

    Put rancours in the vessel of my peace   65

    Only for them, and mine eternal jewel

    Given to the common enemy of man,

    To make them kings, the seeds of Banquo kings!

    Rather than so, come, Fate, into the list,

    And champion me to th'utterance! Who's there?   70

          Re-enter the **Servant** *and two* **Murderers**

    Now go to the door and stay there till we call.

              The **Servant** *goes.*

    Was it not yesterday we spoke together?

First Murderer

    It was, so please your Highness.

Macbeth   Well then, now

    Have you consider'd of my speeches? Know

45 *without* outside.

46–47 *To be...thus* It means nothing to me to be king unless the position is secure.

48 *stick deep* Macbeth compares the threat he feels from Banquo to something sharp sticking into his flesh.

48 *royalty of nature* kingly nature.

50 *to that...mind* in addition to his courageous spirit.

54 *genius* guardian angel or spirit. It was believed that each person was controlled by such a spirit. Macbeth compares the way his own guardian angel is subdued by Banquo's to the way the Roman Mark Anthony's was by Octavius Caesar, the nephew of the great Caesar.

55 *chid* rebuked, defied.

59–60 *fruitless crown, barren sceptre* Macbeth's crown and sceptre cannot be passed on to his own children.

60 *gripe* grasp.

61 *with an unlineal hand* by a hand that is not of my family.

63 *fil'd* defiled.

65 *rancours* bitterness. Macbeth compares the way the murder of Duncan has destroyed his own peace of mind to a chalice of wholesome liquid filled with something bitter.

66 *eternal jewel* his immortal soul.

67 *common enemy of man* the Devil.

68 *seeds of Banquo* Banquo's descendants.

69–70 *come Fate...utterance* Macbeth, using the comparison of a medieval tournament, challenges Fate (the knight) to the tournament (list) to fight him to the death (champion me to th'utterance). In other words, instead of accepting the Witches' words, that Banquo's children will be kings, Macbeth will defy them and, in doing so, defy fate. **How might he do this?**

That it was he, in the times past, which held you 75
So under fortune, which you thought had been
Our innocent self. This I made good to you
In our last conference, pass'd in probation with you,
How you were borne in hand, how cross'd, the instruments,
Who wrought with them, and all things else that might 80
To half a soul and to a notion craz'd
Say, 'Thus did Banquo.'
First Murderer   You made it known to us.
Macbeth
I did so; and went further, which is now
Our point of second meeting. Do you find
Your patience so predominant in your nature 85
That you can let this go? Are you so gospell'd,
To pray for this good man and for his issue,
Whose heavy hand hath bow'd you to the grave
And beggar'd yours for ever?
First Murderer   We are men, my liege.
Macbeth
Ay, in the catalogue ye go for men; 90
As hounds, and greyhounds, mongrels, spaniels, curs,
Shoughs, water-rugs, and demi-wolves, are clept
All by the name of dogs. The valued file
Distinguishes the swift, the slow, the subtle,
The house-keeper, the hunter, every one 95
According to the gift which bounteous nature
Hath in him clos'd; whereby he does receive
Particular addition, from the bill
That writes them all alike; and so of men.
Now, if you have a station in the file, 100
Not i'th'worst rank of manhood, say't;
And I will put that business in your bosoms
Whose execution takes your enemy off,
Grapples you to the heart and love of us,
Who wear our health but sickly in his life, 105
Which in his death were perfect.
Second Murderer   I am one, my liege,
Whom the vile blows and buffets of the world

75–76 *held you...under fortune* held you back in your careers.

78 *pass'd in probation* proved to you to be true.

79 *borne in hand* deceived; *cross'd* frustrated.

79–80 *the instruments...them* the means used and the person using them.

81 *To half...craz'd* to a half-wit and a mad-man.

82 *Thus did Banquo* **What is the effect of keeping this till the end?**

84–86 *Do you...go* Are you so patient that you're prepared to let him get away with this?

86 *gospell'd* so influenced by the teaching of the gospels.

87 *for his issue* **What is Macbeth's real concern?**

89 *beggar'd yours* deprived your children.

89 *We are men* **what does the Murderer imply?**

90 *catalogue* classification list.

92 *shoughs* rough coated shaggy dogs. *water-rugs* rough water dogs. *demi-wolves* half-wolves, a cross between a dog and a wolf. *clept* called.

93 *valued file* the file in which their real qualities are listed.

95 *house-keeper* the guard dog.

97 *hath...clos'd* has endowed him with.

98 *Particular addition* special distinguishing mark.

100–101 *station, rank, file* all these refer to status or position.

102–104 *And I will...love of us* I'll put a piece of business your way which will rid you of your enemy and make you a close friend of mine.

105–106 *Who wear...perfect* Macbeth suggests that his own health is threatened while Banquo lives and only through his death can he begin to be perfectly healthy again.

Hath so incens'd that I am reckless what
I do to spite the world.
First Murderer   And I another,
So weary with disasters, tugg'd with fortune,   110
That I would set my life on any chance,
To mend it or be rid on't.
Macbeth   Both of you
Know Banquo was your enemy.
Both Murderers   True, my lord.
Macbeth
So is he mine; and in such bloody distance
That every minute of his being thrusts   115
Against my near'st of life: and though I could
With bare-fac'd power sweep him from my sight,
And bid my will avouch it, yet I must not,
For certain friends that are both his and mine,
Whose loves I may not drop, but wail his fall   120
Who I myself struck down; and thence it is
That I to your assistance do make love,
Masking the business from the common eye
For sundry weighty reasons.
Second Murderer   We shall, my lord,
Perform what you command us.
First Murderer   Though our lives –   125
Macbeth
Your spirits shine through you. Within this hour at most,
I will advise you where to plant yourselves,
Acquaint you with the perfect spy o'th'time,
The moment on't; for 't must be done tonight,
And something from the palace; always thought   130
That I require a clearness: and with him,
To leave no rubs nor botches in the work,
Fleance, his son, that keeps him company,
Whose absence is no less material to me
Than is his father's, must embrace the fate   135
Of that dark hour. Resolve yourselves apart;
I'll come to you anon.
Both Murderers   We are resolv'd, my lord.

110 *tugg'd* pulled in different directions.

112 *To mend...on't* to improve or to end my life.

114 *bloody* deadly.

115–116 *every minute...life* it is as though every moment he is alive a sword threatens the vital parts of my body.

117 *bare-fac'd power* As King, there is nothing to stop Macbeth from openly using force against Banquo.

118 *bid my will avouch it* kill him just because I want to.

120–121 *but wail his fall...down* instead I must grieve for the loss of the man I killed.

122 *I to your...love* I appeal for your help.

124 *sundry* various.

125 **Notice how Macbeth cuts short the words of the First Murderer. Why does he do this and what is its effect?**

127 *plant* hide.

128–129 *Acquaint...on't* Macbeth indicates that he will advise the Murderers on the best moment for carrying out the deed. It has also been suggested that *the perfect spy o'th'time* could refer to the Third Murderer who appears in scene 3.

130 *something from the palace* well away from the palace.

130–131 *and with...work* bear in mind that at all times I must be free from suspicion.

134 *material* important.

135–136 *must embrace...dark hour* Fleance must die at the same moment.

136 *Resolve yourselves apart* Macbeth gives the men a chance to discuss the matter alone.

Macbeth
I'll call upon you straight: abide within.

The **Murderers** *go*

It is concluded: Banquo, thy soul's flight
If it find heaven must find it out tonight.

He goes

138 *straight* at once.

140

POINTS TO CONSIDER

? 3 *foully* How many people now suspect Macbeth of the murder of Duncan?

? 6–10 What impression of Banquo do you gain in these lines?

? 11–13 What are Macbeth and Lady Macbeth really saying about Banquo here? What tone do they use? What should we begin to suspect at this moment and why?

? 48–52 What qualities does Macbeth recognise in Banquo? Is his assessment of Banquo an accurate one? What is Macbeth's reaction to these qualities?

? 73–89 What new information have we now been given? What means does Macbeth use to influence the Murderers?

? 122–124 What do you think is the real reason for Macbeth hiring the Murderers? Remember that he seemed quite prepared to murder Duncan himself?

ACT THREE SCENE 1 SUGGESTED ACTIVITIES

Production/Group Work

P1 Work in groups of six to eight people. Re-read lines 1–43 of this scene. Then, taking on the roles of the characters involved and the producer of the play, work out how you might stage this part of the scene. Act it out, bearing in mind facial expressions, tone, bearing, stage positions etc. Try to make the attitudes and relationships of one character to another quite clear. In particular, concentrate on each character's attitude to Macbeth and Lady Macbeth.

P2 Imagine that the play is set in the 20th century and the news of the Witches' prophecy has just been leaked to the press. Set up a television interview between Banquo and a TV reporter in which Banquo's present feelings and his part in the incident emerge. Work in pairs and carry out the interviews.

Text

T1a) Re-read Macbeth's speech, lines 46–70. Then, working in pairs and without the text, fill in the words missing from the speech below. (Write your words in a list on a separate sheet of paper, not in the book.) Try to use Shakespeare's original words if you can remember them. If not, use words that seem appropriate to you.

To be thus is _____,
But to be _____ thus. Our fears in Banquo
_____ deep, and in his royalty of nature
Reigns that which would be _____. 'Tis much he dares,
And to that _____ temper of his mind
He hath a wisdom that doth guide his _____
To act in _____. ....
Upon my head they plac'd a _____ crown
And put a _____ sceptre in my gripe,
Thence to be wrench'd with an _____ hand,
No _____ of mine succeeding. If't be so,
For Banquo's _____ have I fil'd my mind;
For them the gracious Duncan have I _____;
Put rancours in the _____ of my peace
Only for them, and mine eternal _____
Given to the common _____ of man,
To make them kings, the _____ of Banquo kings!

b) When you have finished, look at the speech in the text and write down the original words in a list next to your own. Then, with your partner, compare the two lists of words. If you have used different words, discuss with your partner what effect Shakespeare's words convey and how they are different from yours.

c) Working alone and using your own words, describe how Macbeth might feel as he speaks these words.

T2 Add more images to your Image Trees.

Written Work

W1 Look again at lines 14–39 of this scene. Both Banquo and Macbeth are witholding their true thoughts and feelings from each other. Write a paragraph for each character which describes what they are actually thinking as they speak.

W2 Re-write the conversation between Macbeth and the two Murderers. Set it in the 20th century and imagine Macbeth as a gangster. Provide a setting and your own names and details.

SCENE 2

Forres. Another room in the palace.
Enter **Lady Macbeth** *and a Servant.*

Lady Macbeth
Is Banquo gone from court?
Servant
Ay, madam, but returns again tonight.
Lady Macbeth
Say to the King I would attend his leisure
For a few words.
Servant   Madam, I will.

He goes.

Lady Macbeth   Nought's had, all's spent,
Where our desire is got without content.   5
'Tis safer to be that which we destroy,
Than by destruction dwell in doubtful joy.

Enter **Macbeth**

How now, my lord! why do you keep alone,
Of sorriest fancies your companions making,
Using those thoughts which should indeed have died   10
With them they think on? Things without all remedy
Should be without regard; what's done is done.
Macbeth
We have scotch'd the snake, not kill'd it:
She'll close, and be herself, whilst our poor malice
Remains in danger of her former tooth.   15
But let the frame of things disjoint, both the worlds
suffer,
Ere we will eat our meal in fear and sleep
In the affliction of these terrible dreams
That shake us nightly. Better be with the dead,
Whom we, to gain our peace, have sent to peace,   20
Than on the torture of the mind to lie

1 *Is Banquo gone from court?* **why do you think Lady Macbeth asks this question? What may she be thinking?**
3–4 *I would attend...few words* I'd like to speak to him when he has a moment.
4–7 *Nought's had...doubtful joy* we've gained absolutely nothing and lost everything if getting our own way has not brought us happiness. It would be better to be dead like Duncan than be murderers living in constant insecurity.
8 *why do you keep alone?* **What else does this suggest about their relationship?**
9 *sorriest fancies* most depressing thoughts.
10–11 *Using those thoughts...think on* keeping those thoughts in your mind which should have died with Duncan.
13 *scotch'd* wounded, gashed.
14 *close* heal up again.
14–15 *whilst our...former tooth* despite our feeble attempts to harm the snake, we are still threatened by her poisonous tongue. Macbeth uses the venom of the snake to convey the idea of the threats and dangers that surround him. In murdering Duncan, he feels as though he has merely wounded the snake without actually killing it. **Do you think he has something specific in mind when he speaks of the** *snake* **and the** *former tooth***?**
16 *But let...suffer* let the whole world, heaven and earth, collapse. **What do you notice about the length of this line? What is its effect?**
17–19 *Ere we...nightly* **What new information do we learn here? How have we been prepared for it?**
19–20 *Better be...to peace* **Which words do these echo?**
21 The mind is compared here to a rack used to torture the victim.

In restless ecstasy. Duncan is in his grave;
After life's fitful fever he sleeps well;
Treason has done his worst: nor steel, nor poison,
Malice domestic, foreign levy, nothing,
Can touch him further.   25

Lady Macbeth   Come on.
Gentle my lord, sleek o'er your rugged looks;
Be bright and jovial among your guests tonight.

Macbeth
So shall I, love; and so, I pray, be you.
Let your remembrance apply to Banquo;   30
Present him eminence, both with eye and tongue –
Unsafe the while, that we
Must lave our honours in these flattering streams,
And make our faces vizards to our hearts,
Disguising what they are.

Lady Macbeth   You must leave this.   35

Macbeth
O full of scorpions is my mind, dear wife!
Thou know'st that Banquo, and his Fleance, lives.

Lady Macbeth
But in them nature's copy's not eterne.

Macbeth
There's comfort yet; they are assailable;
Then be thou jocund. Ere the bat hath flown   40
His cloister'd flight; ere to black Hecate's summons
The shard-born beetle with his drowsy hums
Hath rung night's yawning peal, there shall be done
A deed of dreadful note.

Lady Macbeth   What's to be done?

Macbeth
Be innocent of the knowledge, dearest chuck,   45
Till thou applaud the deed. Come, seeling night,
Scarf up the tender eye of pitiful day,
And with thy bloody and invisible hand
Cancel and tear to pieces that great bond
Which keeps me pale! Light thickens, and the crow
Makes wing to th' rooky wood;   50
Good things of day begin to droop and drowse,

---

22 *restless ecstasy* constant mental turmoil.

23 *life's fitful fever* he sees life as consisting of a series of bouts of illness.

25 *foreign levy* armies gathered against him from abroad.

27 *sleek...looks* smooth your furrowed brow, (or as we might say, stop worrying). Notice how Lady Macbeth is asking Macbeth once more to put on a composed expression despite his inner turmoil.

30 *Let your...Banquo* pay particular attention to Banquo. **Why does Macbeth say this when he has just planned to murder Banquo?**

32–34 *Unsafe the while...what they are* while we're so insecure, we've got to protect our own positions as King and Queen by flattering other people, (as though washing away suspicion in a stream) and hide our true thoughts by disguising them. A *vizard* is a mask or helmet that covers the face.

36 *scorpions* **What does this single word convey of Macbeth's state of mind?**

38 *But in them...eterne* but Nature has not got the copyright on them. In other words, some day they must die. **Why do you think Lady Macbeth says this?**

39 *assailable* can be attacked.

40 *jocund* joyful.

Notice Macbeth's *comfort* and *jocund*. Why has his mood changed so suddenly?

41 *cloister'd flight* The bat generally lives in dark, lonely places. *black Hecate's summons* As goddess of Witchcraft, Hecate would call upon others by night.

42 *shard* dung.

43 *night's yawning peal* the curfew bell which rings at bed time.

45 *dearest chuck* **What is the effect of this phrase? Why does Macbeth not tell Lady Macbeth exactly what is going on?**

46 *seeling* blinding. In hunting, a falcon's eyelids used to be *seeled* by passing thread through them. This was done to tame it.

46–50 *Come seeling...pale* Macbeth calls upon night to provide a cover for the sore eyes of day so that his terrible crime will be hidden.

49–50 *great bond...pale* the Witches' prophecy, which gives the throne to Banquo's family, and keeps me fenced in. The *pale* was a boundary line.

While's night's black agents to their preys do rouse.
Thou marvell'st at my words: but hold thee still;
Things bad begun make strong themselves by ill.   **55**
So, prithee, go with me.

                                    They leave.

55 *Things bad...ill* One crime leads to another. What outcome of the murder is Macbeth only now beginning to understand?

POINTS TO CONSIDER

? 3–4 Do these words indicate any change in the relationship between Lady Macbeth and Macbeth?

? 4–7 Which words in the previous scene do these recall? In what ways have Macbeth and Lady Macbeth been similarly affected by the murder of Duncan?

? 11–12 *Things without...is done* Which earlier words do these recall? Do you think Lady Macbeth believes what she says?

? 16 What impression is given here of Macbeth's state of mind?

? 23 Notice how often illness or disease is mentioned from here until the end of the play? How are images of disease or illness appropriate in *Macbeth*?

? 27 Which earlier line does this echo?

? 40–44 What world does Macbeth once more inhabit? Which words create the atmosphere of this world? Which lines in an earlier scene do these recall?

? 46–50 When did Macbeth earlier say something similar?

ACT THREE SCENE 2 SUGGESTED ACTIVITIES

Production/Group Work

P1 In small groups of three or four, discuss how you, as producer of the play, might show the audience the changes that have taken place in the relationship between Lady Macbeth and Macbeth.

P2 Working in pairs, take on the roles of a husband or wife who have shared a devastating experience and yet find it difficult to talk about. Invent your own details.

Text

T1 Many of the phrases and images of this scene recall those used earlier in the play. Draw two columns and list phrases or images from this scene in the first and similar ones from elsewhere in the play in the second.

T2a) Re-read lines 46–55 of the scene. Then, working in pairs but without the text, fill in the words missing from the speech below. (Write your words in a list on a separate sheet of paper, not in the book.) Try to use Shakespeare's original words if you can remember them. If not, use words that seem appropriate to you.

Come _____ night,

_____ up the tender eye of pitiful _____,

And with thy _____ and invisible hand

Cancel and _____ to pieces that great bond

Which keeps me _____! Light thickens, and the crow

Makes wing to the _____ wood;

_____ things of day begin to droop and drowse,

Whiles night's _____ agents to their preys do rouse.

Thou _____ at my words: but hold thee still;

Things _____ begun make _____ themselves by ill.

b) When you have finished, look at the speech in the text and write down the original words in a list next to your own. Now, with your partner, compare two lists of words. If you have used different words, discuss with your partner what effect Shakespeare's words convey and how they are different from yours.

c) Working on your own and, making reference to the whole speech, write down what contrasts are drawn here between night and day.

T3 Add more images to your Image Trees.

Written

W1 Lady Macbeth is clearly worried by Macbeth's behaviour and yet she is probably unable to share her concerns with anyone else. If she were living in the 20th century she could write anonymously to the agony column of a magazine. Write the letter that she might have sent.

W2 Lady Macbeth has been compared to the Witches. Is it a fair comparison? Consider their similarities (and differences) and then write them down by using a table similar to the one below. Find a quotation from the play for each point you make. One example has been done for you.

SIMILARITIES		DIFFERENCES	
LADY MACBETH	*WITCHES*	*LADY MACBETH*	*WITCHES*
Tries to deny her own sex: "unsex me here" i–5	Their sex is unclear "You should be women And yet your beards…" i–3		

SCENE 3

Forres. A road leading to the palace.
Enter three **Murderers.**

First Murderer
    Who did bid thee join with us?
Third Murderer   Macbeth.
Second Murderer
    He needs not our mistrust, since he delivers
    Our offices, and what we have to do,
    To the direction just.
First Murderer   Then stand with us.
    The west yet glimmers with some streaks of day;

5

A road leading to the palace. How might the Murderers conceal themselves?

2–4 *He needs…direction just* we don't need to be suspicious of him since he's brought us instructions and how to carry them out just as Macbeth said he would.
6 *lated traveller* one travelling late in the day.
5–7 What use is Shakespeare making here of the First Murderer?

Now spurs the lated traveller apace
To gain the timely inn; and near approaches
The subject of our watch.
Third Murderer   Hark! I hear horses.
Banquo (*not yet in sight*)
Give us a light there, ho!
Second Murderer   Then 'tis he; the rest
That are within the note of expectation   10
Already are i'th'court.
First Murderer   His horses go about.
Third Murderer
Almost a mile; but he does usually,
So all men do, from hence to th'palace gate
Make it their walk.

Enter **Banquo,** *and* **Fleance** *with a torch*

Second Murderer   A light, a light!
Third Murderer   'Tis he.
First Murderer
Stand to 't.   15
Banquo
It will rain tonight.
First Murderer   Let it come down.

The First Murderer puts out the light, while the others attack Banquo.

Banquo
O, treachery! Fly, good Fleance, fly, fly, fly!
Thou may'st revenge. O slave!

He dies. **Fleance** *escapes.*

Third Murderer
Who did strike out the light?
First Murderer   Was't not the way?
Third Murderer
There's but one down; the son is fled.
Second Murderer   We have lost   20

8 *subject of our watch* **Who is referred to?**
10 *within the note of expectation* among those expected at the banquet.
11 *go about* a long way round.
12–14 *but he does...walk* **What does this knowledge suggest about the Third Murderer?**
15 *Stand to 't* get ready to do the deed.
16 *It will rain tonight* **What tone will Banquo use here?**
17 *Let it come down* the First Murderer refers to raining blows, playing on Banquo's words.
19 *the way* the right thing to do.
21 *Best half* **Why does the Second Murderer say this? What is the significance of Fleance's escape?**

Best half of our affair.
First Murderer   Well, let's away,
And say how much is done.

They go

POINTS TO CONSIDER

? *Three Murderers* Why do you think a Third Murderer has appeared? What does it suggest about Macbeth's state of mind?

? 16 What impression does Shakespeare give of Banquo at this particular moment?

? 17 What is the effect of humour at this moment?

ACT THREE SCENE 3 SUGGESTED ACTIVITIES

Production/Group Work

P1 In groups of four, discuss Banquo's character. Should he have realised sooner that his life was in danger? Is there any similarity between his character and Duncan's? Would he have made a good king?

Text

T1 Re-read line 15 to the end of the scene. How has Shakespeare made use of the rhythm of the lines to reflect the action?

Written Work

W1 When famous or well known people die, the newspapers often print a short history of their life or times, an indication of their character and their major achievements. These accounts are called obituaries. Write an obituary on Banquo as it might appear in a modern newspaper. You will find it helpful before you start writing to read some actual examples of obituaries from recent newspapers.

W2 Macbeth must have had a conversation with the Third Murderer prior to this scene. Write out the conversation as you imagine it might have been.

SCENE 4

Forres. A banqueting hall in the palace.
The banquet has been prepared. Enter **Macbeth, Lady Macbeth, Ross,**
Lennox, Lords and Attendants.

Macbeth
> You know your own degrees, sit down; at first
> And last the hearty welcome.

Lords
> Thanks to your Majesty.

Macbeth
> Ourself will mingle with society
> And play the humble host.   5
> Our hostess keeps her state; but in best time
> We will require her welcome.

Lady Macbeth
> Pronounce it for me, sir, to all our friends;
> For my heart speaks they are welcome.

Enter **First Murderer** *at the door.*

Macbeth
> See, they encounter thee with their hearts' thanks.   10
> Both sides are even: here I'll sit i'th' midst.
> Be large in mirth; anon we'll drink a measure
> The table round. (*He goes to the door*)
> There's blood upon thy face.

Murderer   'Tis Banquo's then.

Macbeth
> 'Tis better thee without than he within.   15
> Is he dispatch'd?

Murderer   My lord, his throat is cut;
> That I did for him.

Macbeth   Thou art the best o'th'cut-throats;
> Yet he's good that did the like for Fleance.
> If thou didst it, thou art the nonpareil.

Murderer
> Most royal sir – Fleance is 'scap'd.   20

A large table would probably be laid for the banquet with thrones for Macbeth and Lady Macbeth.

1 *degrees* social ranks in terms of importance. These would decide who sat where. The noblest would sit nearest to the King.

1–2 *at first/And last* from the beginning of the evening to the end.

4 *society* the assembled company.

6 *keeps her state* Lady Macbeth will remain on her throne.

6 *best time* at the appropriate moment.

7 *her welcome* her welcome to you.

10 *encounter thee* greet you. **How will they do this**?

11 *both sides are even* there are the same number of people sitting at each side of the table.

12 *Be large with mirth* enjoy yourselves.

12 *a measure* a large goblet of wine which would be passed round the table for each guest to taste.

Going to the door **How might Macbeth do this without arousing suspicion?**

15 *'tis better...within* his blood is better outside your face than inside Banquo's body.

16 *dispatch'd* killed.

19 *the nonpareil* without an equal.

20 How will the Murderer speak these words?

Macbeth
Then comes my fit again: I had else been perfect,
Whole as the marble, founded as the rock,
As broad and general as the casing air:
But now I am cabin'd, cribb'd, confin'd, bound in
To saucy doubts and fears. But Banquo's safe?   25

Murderer
Ay, my good lord. Safe in a ditch he bides,
With twenty trenched gashes on his head,
The least a death to nature.

Macbeth   Thanks for that.
There the grown serpent lies; the worm that's fled
Hath nature that in time will venom breed,   30
No teeth for th' present. Get thee gone; tomorrow
We'll hear ourselves again.

                    The Murderer goes

Lady Macbeth   My royal lord,
You do not give the cheer: the feast is sold
That is not often vouch'd, while 'tis a-making,
'Tis given with welcome. To feed were best at home: 35
From thence the sauce to meat is ceremony;
Meeting were bare without it.

        Enter the **Ghost of Banquo** *and sits in* **Macbeth's** *place.*

Macbeth   Sweet remembrancer!
Now good digestion wait on appetite,
And health on both!

Lennox   May it please your Highness sit?

Macbeth
Here had we now our country's honour roof'd,   40
Were the grac'd person of our Banquo present;
Who may I rather challenge for unkindness
Than pity for mischance!

Ross   His absence, sir,
Lays blame upon his promise. Please 't your Highness
To grace us with your royal company.   45

Macbeth
The table's full.

21 *fit* fit of anxiety or fear. **How might Macbeth show this?**
perfect completely safe.
22 *whole* solid; *founded* securely based.
23 *as broad...air* as free as the air around us.
24–25 *cabin'd...fears* imprisoned in a small space and prone to nagging doubts and fears.
27 *trenched* deeply cut.
28 *The least ...nature* the smallest of which would have killed a man.
29 *worm* another word for snake. **Who does it refer to?**
30–31 *Hath nature...present* even though he is harmless at the moment, he has the power to become a poisonous snake. **What does he feel might happen in the future?**
32 *We'll hear ourselves again* we'll talk again. **What about?**
33 *the cheer* the toast.
33–35 *the feast...welcome* unless guests are frequently made to feel welcome during the meal, they might just as well have paid for it themselves.
35–37 *To feed...without it* if you just want to eat, you might as well stay at home. If you're away from home, what gives a special flavour to the meal is the style and ceremony that goes with it. Without it, the occasion would be a dull one.
Enter the Ghost of Banquo The stage directions suggest that the audience could see the Ghost a few moments earlier than Macbeth. What effect would this create?
37 *Sweet remembrancer* a timely reminder. Macbeth politely thanks Lady Macbeth for recalling him to his duties to his guests. **Which of her earlier instructions is he carrying out at present?**
40 *country's honour* the most noble man in the country. **Who is he referring to?**
roof'd under our roof.
42–43 *Who may...mischance* Macbeth hopes that it is bad manners rather than bad luck that have kept Banquo away.
44 *Lays blame...promise* he's in the wrong for having promised to come.

Lennox   Here's a place reserv'd, sir.
Macbeth
    Where?
Lennox   Here, my good lord.
    What is't that moves your Highness?
Macbeth
    Which of you have done this?
Lords   What, my good lord?
Macbeth
    Thou canst not say I did it: never shake   50
    Thy gory locks at me.
Ross
    Gentlemen, rise; his Highness is not well.
Lady Macbeth
    Sit, worthy friends. My lord is often thus,
    And hath been from his youth. Pray you, keep seat;
    The fit is momentary; upon a thought   55
    He will again be well. If much you note him,
    You shall offend him and extend his passion.
    Feed, and regard him not. – Are you a man?
Macbeth
    Ay, and a bold one that dare look on that
    Which might appal the devil.
Lady Macbeth   O proper stuff!   60
    This is the very painting of your fear;
    This is the air-drawn dagger which, you said,
    Led you to Duncan. O, these flaws and starts –
    Imposters to true fear – would well become
    A woman's story at a winter's fire,   65
    Authoris'd by her grandam. Shame itself!
    Why do you make such faces? When all's done,
    You look but on a stool.
Macbeth   Prithee see there!
    Behold! look! lo! how say you?
    Why, what care I? If thou canst nod, speak too.   70
    If charnel-houses and our graves must send
    Those that we bury back, our monuments
    Shall be the maws of kites. (*The Ghost disappears*)

48 *What is't that moves your Highness?* **what now becomes apparent?** In his *Daemonologie*, James I had written that ghosts came to demand vengeance and could only be seen by the guilty.
49 *Which...done this* **What does Macbeth suspect?**
50 *Thou canst not say I did it* **Has Macbeth any justification for saying this**?
51 *gory locks* **What does this suggest about Banquo's appearance**?
53–54 *Sit...seat* **What is Lady Macbeth doing here?**
55 *upon a thought* in a moment.
56 *note* take notice.
60 *O proper stuff!* nonsense!
61 *painting of your fear* not real fear, but the result of you imagination. Lady Macbeth compares this episode with the vision of the dagger which she saw as 'air-drawn' and therefore not real.
63 *flaws and starts* outbursts.
64 *imposters to true fear* unreal when compared with true fear.
66 *Authoris'd...grandam* old wives' tales told originally by her grandmother.
69 *Behold!...you* **What do you think might be happening at this moment?**
71 *charnel-houses* tombs.
72–73 *our monuments...kites* the only tombs we'll be able to use will be the stomachs of kites. Kites were birds of prey which would, of course, swoop down on dead flesh.
maws stomachs.

Lady Macbeth   What! quite unmann'd in folly?
Macbeth
    If I stand here, I saw him.
Lady Macbeth   Fie! for shame!
Macbeth
    Blood hath been shed ere now, i'th'olden time,   75
    Ere humane statute purg'd the gentle weal;
    Ay, and since too, murders have been perform'd
    Too terrible for the ear. The time has been
    That when the brains were out, the man would die,
    And there an end; but now they rise again,   80
    With twenty mortal murders on their crowns,
    And push us from our stools. This is more strange
    Than such a murder is.
Lady Macbeth   My worthy lord,
    Your noble friends do lack you.
Macbeth   I do forget.
    Do not muse at me, my most worthy friends;   85
    I have a strange infirmity, which is nothing
    To those that know me. Come, love and health to all;
    Then I'll sit down. Give me some wine: fill full.

             The Ghost *enters.*

    I drink to the general joy o'th' whole table,
    And to our dear friend Banquo, whom we miss;   90
    Would he were here! To all, and him, we thirst,
    And all to all.
Lords   Our duties, and the pledge.
Macbeth
    Avaunt! and quit my sight! Let the earth hide thee!
    Thy bones are marrowless, thy blood is cold;
    Thou hast no speculation in those eyes   95
    Which thou dost glare with!
Lady Macbeth   Think of this, good peers,
    But as a thing of custom: 'tis no other;
    Only it spoils the pleasure of the time.
Macbeth
    What man dare, I dare:

73 *unmann'd in folly* has all your courage been completely destroyed by this foolishness? **What is Lady Macbeth doing here?**

75–76 *Blood...weal* there was plenty of bloodshed before the laws of society civilized this country.

8–081 *but now...crowns* now the dead has come back to life with twenty fatal wounds in his head. **Which earlier words does the phrase *twenty fatal wounds* recall?** It was believed at the time that ghosts bled if they confronted their killer.

85 *muse* be astonished.

91 *all to all* we will drink to each other.

92 *Our duties and the pledge* the lords offer their oath of allegiance.

93 *avaunt* get away.

95 *speculation* visible signs of intelligence. **What sort of expression will Banquo have in his eyes?**

97 *thing of custom* something that often happens.

How will Lady Macbeth's excuses now appear to the assembled group?

Approach thou like the rugged Russian bear,
The arm'd rhinoceros, or th'Hyrcan tiger; 100
Take any shape but that, and my firm nerves
Shall never tremble: or be alive again,
And dare me to the desert with thy sword;
If trembling I inhabit, then protest me 105
The baby of a girl. Hence, horrible shadow!
Unreal mock'ry, hence!

The **Ghost** *vanishes.*

Why, so; being gone,
I am a man again. Pray you, sit still.

Lady Macbeth
You have displac'd the mirth, broke the good meeting,
With most admir'd disorder.

Macbeth   Can such things be, 110
And overcome us like a summer's cloud,
Without our special wonder? You make me strange
Even to the disposition that I owe,
When now I think you can behold such sights
And keep the natural ruby of your cheeks, 115
When mine is blanch'd with fear.

Ross   What sights, my lord?

Lady Macbeth
I pray you speak not; he grows worse and worse;
Question enrages him. At once, good night:
Stand not upon the order of your going,
But go at once.

Lennox   Good night; and better health 120
Attend his Majesty!

Lady Macbeth   A kind good night to all!

The **Lords and Attendants** *leave.*

Macbeth
It will have blood; they say blood will have blood.
Stones have been known to move, and trees to speak;
Augurs and understood relations have
By maggot-pies and choughs and rooks brought forth 125
The secret'st man of blood. What is the night?

101 *arm'd* with thick hide and tusks, like a sword and armour. *Hyrcan tiger* particularly fierce tigers from Hircania in Persia.

104 *dare* challenge.

105–106 *If trembling...girl* if I show any signs of fear, then you can call me a baby.

107 *being gone* now it has gone.

109–110 *You have...disorder* you have spoilt all the fun of the occasion with your amazing lack of control.

111 *overcome us* pass over us.

112 *without our special wonder* with no more surprise from us than that we might show at a summer's cloud.

112–113 *You make...I owe* you make me feel a stranger to myself.

116 *blanch'd* turned pale.

117–118 *I pray...him* **Why does Lady Macbeth say this**?

119 *Stand not...going* just leave the table in any order.

122 *they say...blood* murder demands vengeance with the death of the murderer.

123 *Stones...speak* in order to reveal the hidden body of the murderer's victim.

124–126 *Augurs...blood* the flights of certain birds have revealed omens and divinations (an understanding of omens). The Elizabethans were superstitious and, like the Romans, believed that there were a certain established set of good and bad omens which warned of good or bad deeds. These sometimes related to the particular flight paths of birds. *at odds* in dispute.

What point in the play does this moment mark?

Lady Macbeth
Almost at odds with morning, which is which.
Macbeth
How say'st thou that Macduff denies his person
At our great bidding?
Lady Macbeth   Did you send to him, sir?
Macbeth
I hear it by the way; but I will send.   130
There's not a one of them but in his house
I keep a servant fee'd. I will tomorrow,
And betimes I will, to the Weird Sisters:
More shall they speak; for now I am bent to know,
By the worst means, the worst. For mine own good   135
All causes shall give way. I am in blood
Stepp'd in so far that, should I wade no more,
Returning were as tedious as go o'er.
Strange things I have in head that will to hand,
Which must be acted ere they may be scann'd.   140
Lady Macbeth
You lack the season of all natures, sleep.
Macbeth
Come, we'll to sleep. My strange and self-abuse
Is the initiate fear that wants hard use.
We are yet young in deed.

        They go.

128–129 *denies...bidding* refuses to accept my invitation.

I will tomorrow I'll deal with that tomorrow. **How?**

133 *betimes* without delay.

134 *bent* determined.

135 *By the worst means the worst* **what aspect of the Witches does Macbeth now fully recognise?**

135–136 *For mine...way* all other considerations must give way to what I want.

138 *tedious* as much trouble.

139–140 *Strange things...season'd* I have many strange things to do which must be done without being thought about too carefully in advance.

141 *season* seasoning, used at the time to keep food fresh. Another confirmation here that Macbeth and Lady Macbeth cannot sleep.

142–143 *My strange...use* the delusions I am suffering from (in seeing the ghost) are simply the fears of an inexperienced beginner.

144 *young* inexperienced.

POINTS TO CONSIDER

? 16 *dispatch'd* Why does Macbeth use this word rather than *killed*?

? 40–44 What effect does Shakespeare achieve in these lines? What are your feelings towards Macbeth at this moment?

? 52 Ross is the first to respond to the situation. How does this fit in with what we already know of him?

? 58 *Are you a man?* When did Lady Macbeth last speak like this?

? 119 Compare this with lines 1–2. What does it suggest about the significance of this whole episode? See earlier notes on *Killing a King*.

? 127 *Almost...which* what tone of voice will Lady Macbeth use here? What has happened to her now all her guests have gone? What does this suggest about her own state during the banquet?

? 131 What insight does this information give us into Macbeth's own state of mind? What sort of man has he now become?

? 133 Why does Macbeth need to see the Weird Sisters? What is their importance to him now?

? 136–138 What image does Macbeth make use of in these lines? Does it help you understand what he is saying?

? 139–140 When did Macbeth last think carefully before acting? Why does he not want to do so now? What do you think the *strange things* might be?

ACT THREE SCENE 4 SUGGESTED ACTIVITIES

Production/Group Work

Work in groups of about six or seven for the following three exercises. Before you start, assign the roles of Macbeth, Lady Macbeth, Ross, Lennox, Murderer, Producer and, if possible, a Lord to people in each group.

P1 Draw a diagram of the stage and agree amongst yourselves where each guest will sit at the table. Draw in other details of the stage that might be needed in the course of the scene.

P2 Obtain a photocopy of the scene and write in detailed stage directions and production notes for actors taking part in it. Pay particular attention to facial expressions, Macbeth's movements, asides between Macbeth and Lady Macbeth. Finally, discuss whether or not the Ghost of Banquo should actually appear on the stage.

P3 Mime the scene. Then discuss what has been gained and what has been lost by such an approach.

Text

T1 In pairs, pick out as many examples of dramatic irony as you can find. (See notes on *Style* on p 00). What effect does Shakespeare achieve through these?

T2 Add more images to your Image Trees.

Written Work

W1 Imagine that Ross and Lennox meet after this to discuss the banquet. Make up the conversation they might have had.

W2 The Servants would no doubt have to return all the uneaten food to the kitchens. They might also have been aware of some of the strange events taking place in the banqueting hall. Write a humorous dialogue between a servant and the cook who has prepared the banquet.

SCENE 5

An open space on a moor. Thunder.
Enter the three **Witches,** *meeting* **Hecate.**

First Witch
    Why, how now, Hecate! You look angerly.
Hecate
    Have I not reason, beldams as you are,
    Saucy and overbold? How did you dare
    To trade and traffic with Macbeth
    In riddles and affairs of death;   5
    And I, the mistress of your charms,
    The close contriver of all harms,
    Was never call'd to bear my part,
    Or show the glory of our art?
    And, which is worse, all you have done   10
    Hath been but for a wayward son,
    Spiteful and wrathful; who, as others do,
    Loves for his own ends, not for you.
    But make amends now: get you gone,
    And at the pit of Acheron   15
    Meet me i'the morning: thither he
    Will come to know his destiny.
    Your vessels and your spells provide,
    Your charms, and everything beside.
    I am for th'air; this night I'll spend   20
    Unto a dismal and a fatal end.
    Great business must be wrought ere noon.
    Upon the corner of the moon
    There hangs a vap'rous drop profound;
    I'll catch it ere it come to ground: 25
    And that, distill'd by magic sleights,
    Shall raise such artificial sprites
    As, by the strength of their illusion,
    Shall draw him on to his confusion.
    He shall spurn fate, scorn death, and bear   30
    His hopes 'bove wisdom, grace, and fear;

The setting is similar to the first scene.

1 *angerly* angry.
2 *beldams* hags.
3 *traffic* deal.
6 *charms* powers.
7 *close contriver* secret designer.
harms evil deeds.
8 *art* the art of witchcraft.
11 *wayward son* **Who is this?**
12–13 *who...you* Macbeth makes use of evil for his own ends, not because he loves evil in itself.
15 *pit of Acheron* here the name given to the Witches' cavern in some infernal region. In classical legend it was a river in the Greek underworld.
21 *Unto...end* on a disastrous and ominous mission.
23–24 *Upon...profound* the moon was supposed to shed a deep, pear-shaped dew drop of liquid upon certain herbs and plants. This liquid had magical qualities and was therefore sought after.
26 *sleights* tricks, arts.
27 *artificial sprites* spirits or ghosts conjured up by magic.
29 *confusion* ruin or damnation.
30–31 *bear...fear* his ambition will make him blind to reason, religion and natural fear. **Where did his 'hopes' come from?**
32 *security* complacency, overconfidence.
'Come away' a song from another play by Thomas Middleton, a contemporary playwright of Shakespeare.

And you all know security
Is mortals' chiefest enemy.
(*Music and a song within*: 'Come away, come away.')
Hark! I am call'd; my little spirit, see,
Sits in a foggy cloud, and stays for me.   **35**

She goes

First Witch
Come, let's make haste; she'll soon be back again.

They go.

POINTS TO CONSIDER

? What is the effect of the appearance of the Witches on the audience now?

? 30 *He shall spurn fate* We have already seen Macbeth do this. When?

? 34 *little spirit* What does this refer to? (see notes on The Weird Sisters p 9)

? What important clues does Hecate give us to Macbeth's future?

ACT THREE SCENE 5 SUGGESTED ACTIVITIES

Text

It is generally felt that Shakespeare did not write this scene. In small groups of two or three, discuss the following:

T1 Look closely at the scene. What clues are there that it might not have been written by the person who wrote the other Witches' scenes?

T2 This scene is often omitted from productions of the play. What would be lost without it?

T3 Can you think of any reason why this scene may have been added to the play at a later date by someone else?

SCENE 6

Forres. The palace.
Enter **Lennox** *and another* **Lord.**

Lennox

My former speeches have but hit your thoughts,
Which can interpret farther: only I say
Things have been strangely borne. The gracious Duncan
Was pitied of Macbeth. Marry, he was dead.
And the right-valiant Banquo walk'd too late;   5
Whom, you may say, if't please you, Fleance kill'd,
For Fleance fled. Men must not walk too late.
Who cannot want the thought, how monstrous
It was for Malcolm and for Donalbain
To kill their gracious father? Damned fact!   10
How it did grieve Macbeth! Did he not straight,
In pious rage, the two delinquents tear,
That were the slaves of drink and thralls of sleep?
Was not that nobly done? Ay, and wisely too;
For 'twould have anger'd any heart alive   15
To hear the men deny't. So that, I say,
He has borne all things well; and I do think
That had he Duncan's sons under his key –
As, an't please heaven, he shall not – they should find
What 'twere to kill a father; so should Fleance.   20
But peace! For from broad word, and 'cause he fail'd
His presence at the tyrant's feast, I hear,
Macduff lives in disgrace. Sir, can you tell
Where he bestows himself?

Lord   The son of Duncan,
From whom this tyrant holds the due of birth,   25
Lives in the English court, and is receiv'd
Of the most pious Edward with such grace
That the malevolence of fortune nothing
Takes from his high respect. Thither Macduff
Is gone to pray the holy King upon his aid   30
To wake Northumberland and warlike Siward:

We now see the action from the point of view of Lennox.

1–2 *My former...farther* I have only been saying what you've been thinking. Now you can draw your own conclusions. **What does *former speeches* suggest?**
2 *strangely borne* handled rather oddly.
3–4 *The gracious...dead* Macbeth only pitied Duncan when it was safe for him to do so, ie after he was dead.
6–7 *Whom...fled* The same argument could apply to Fleance as to Malcolm and Donalbain, that because he fled, he had killed his father. **What tone of voice is Lennox using?**
10 *fact* crime, deed.
11 *straight* immediately.
13 *thralls* captives.
15–16 *For 'twould...deny't* **what does Lennox really mean?**
19 *an't* if it.
19–20 *they should find...Fleance* they would all be taught a lesson for killing their fathers!
21 *broad word* because Macduff was outspoken.
22 *tyrant's* **What is the relationship now between Macbeth and his Lords?**
24 *bestows* lives.
25 *holds the due of birth* prevents him from taking the Scottish crown.
27 *pious Edward* Edward, who ruled England from 1042–1066, was known as Edward the Confessor and was deeply religious.
28–29 *That the malevolence...respect* his misfortune has not lost him any honour.
30 *the holy king* see *pious* above. **What contrast is implied?**
30 *upon his aid* on behalf of Malcolm.
31 *wake Northumberland...Siward* call the Earl of Northumberland and Siward, his son, to arms.

That by the help of these – with Him above
To ratify the work – we may again
Give to our tables meat, sleep to our nights,
Free from our feasts and banquets bloody knives,   35
Do faithful homage and receive free honours;
All which we pine for now. And this report
Hath so exasperate the King that he
Prepares for some attempt of war.
Lennox   Sent he to Macduff?
Lord
He did: and with an absolute 'Sir, not I!'   40
The cloudy messenger turns me his back
And hums, as who should say 'You'll rue the time
That clogs me with this answer'.
Lennox   And that well might
Advise him to a caution t'hold what distance
His wisdom can provide. Some holy angel   45
Fly to the court of England and unfold
His message ere he come, that a swift blessing
May soon return to this our suffering country
Under a hand accurs'd!
Lord   I'll send my prayers with him.

They go

33 *To ratify the work* to sanction their activities.
35 *Free...knives* keep our feasts and banquets free of violence.
36 *Do faithful homage* pay our loyal respects.
38 *exasperate* exasperated, angered.
39 *attempt of war* **What picture of Macbeth does Lennox give?**
40 *'Sir, not I'* Macduff's flat refusal to come.
41 *cloudy...back* the sullen messenger turned his back on Macduff.
42–43 *'You'll rue...answer'* you'll regret the day you lumbered me with this reply.
43–45 *And that...provide* if he is wise, he should take it as a warning to keep well away from Macbeth.
47 *His* Macduff's.
What note does this scene end on?

POINTS TO CONSIDER

? When did we last see Lennox? What is the importance of his view of recent events?

? 6–7 What do we now learn from the tone Lennox adopts in this speech? Is there any other reason for Lennox to use this tone apart from his own cynicism?

ACT THREE SCENE 6 SUGGESTED ACTIVITIES

Production/Group Work

P1 Working in pairs, mark any examples of irony in Lennox's speech. Then read the scene aloud, taking a part each. Use tone and gesture as fully as you can to convey the idea that you know a lot more than you can actually say, but that it would be dangerous to say any more.

Text

T1a) Re-read lines 24–39 of the scene. Then, working in pairs but without the text, fill in the words missing from the speech below. (Write your words in a list on a separate sheet of paper, not in the book.) Try to use Shakespeare's original words if you can remember them. If not, use words that seem appropriate to you.

The son of Duncan,
From whom this _____ holds the due of birth,
Lives in the _____ court, and is receiv'd
Of the most _____ Edward with such _____
That malevolence of _____ nothing
Takes from his high _____. Thither Macduff
Is gone to pray the _____ King upon his _____
To wake Northumberland and _____ Siward:
That by the help of these – with _____ above
To _____ the work – we may again
Give to our tables _____, _____ to our nights,
Free from our feasts and banquets _____ _____,
Do _____ homage and receive free honours;
All which we _____ for now. And this report
Hath so _____ the King that he
Prepares for some attempt of _____.

b) When you have finished, look at the speech in the text and write down the original words in a list next to your own. With your partner, compare the two lists of words. If you have used different words, discuss what effect Shakespeare's words convey and how they are different from yours.

c) Working on your own and using Shakespeare's original words (from your second list) write down briefly what impression these words give of the contrasts between England and Scotland.

T2 Add more images to your Image Trees.

Written

W1 Look back at the part played by Lennox in the play so far. When do you think he first became suspicious of Macbeth? Imagine that he has kept a diary of the events of the play so far. Reproduce extracts of that diary to give an indication of his own changing attitude to Macbeth.

Act Four

SCENE 1

A dark cavern on the moor. In the middle is a cauldron boiling.
Thunder. Enter the three Witches

First Witch
Thrice the brinded cat hath mew'd.
Second Witch
Thrice and once the hedge-pig whin'd.
Third Witch
Harpier cries: 'tis time, 'tis time.
First Witch
Round about the cauldron go;
In the poison'd entrails throw.   5
Toad that under cold stone
Days and nights has thirty-one
Swelter'd venom sleeping got,
Boil thou first i th' charmed pot.
All
Double, double toil and trouble;   10
Fire burn, and cauldron bubble.
Second Witch
Fillet of a fenny snake,
In the cauldron boil and bake;
Eye of newt, and toe of frog,
Wool of bat, and tongue of dog,   15
Adder's fork, and blind-worm's sting,
Lizard's leg, and howlet's wing,
For a charm of powerful trouble,
Like a hell-broth boil and bubble.

The cavern had earlier been described as *the pit of Acheron*. **What is the effect of a boiling cauldron in the centre of the stage?**

1 *brinded* brown streaked with other colours. She is referring to her familiar. (See notes on the *Weird Sisters* p.9.)
2 *hedge-pig* hedgehog. The Second Witch's familiar.
3 *Harpier* her familiar and probably related to a harpy, a monster in Greek mythology which had a woman's face and body and a bird's wings and claws.
6 *Toad . . . stone* **What effect is created by the words used here?**
8 *Swelter'd venom* sweated poison.
4–9 What have these ingredients in common?
12 *fillet* slice. *fenny* from the fens, which were bog or marshland.
16 *Adder's fork* forked tongue. *blindworm's sting* at the time, it was believed to have a poisonous sting.
17 *howlet's wing* owlet's wing. An owlet is a baby owl.
19 *Like a hell-broth* **What is the Second Witch trying to do to the brew?**
12–19 What have these ingredients in common?

All
Double, double toil and trouble;   20
Fire burn, and cauldron bubble.

Third Witch
Scale of dragon, tooth of wolf,
Witch's mummy, maw and gulf
Of the ravin'd salt-sea shark,
Root of hemlock digg'd i'th'dark,   25
Liver of blaspheming Jew,
Gall of goat, and slips of yew
Sliver'd in the moon's eclipse,
Nose of Turk, and Tartar's lips,
Finger of birth-strangled babe   30
Ditch-deliver'd by a drab,
Make the gruel thick and slab;
Add thereto a tiger's chaudron,
For the ingredience of our cauldron.

All
Double, double toil and trouble;   35
Fire burn, and cauldron bubble.

Second Witch
Cool it with a baboon's blood,
Then the charm is firm and good.

                          Enter Hecate

Hecate
O well done! I commend your pains;
And every one shall share i'th'gains.   40
And now about the cauldron sing,
Like elves and fairies in a ring,
Enchanting all that you put in.

            (*Music and a song, 'Black Spirits'. Hecate goes*)

Second Witch
By the pricking in my thumbs,
Something wicked this way comes. (*Knocking*)   45
Open, locks,
Whoever knocks.

23 *Witch's mummy* medicine made from the flesh of a witch's body. *maw and gulf* throat and stomach.
24 *ravin'd* glutted or crammed with its prey.
25 *Root of hemlock . . . dark* a poisonous herb, made even more potent if dug up at night.
27 *slips of yew* cuttings taken from a yew tree. These were also poisonous.
28 *sliver'd* sliced off. *moon's eclipse* a time of ill omen.
29 *Turk, Tartar* they were felt at the time to be both unchristian and extremely cruel.
31 *Ditch . . . drab* born in a ditch to a prostitute.
32 *slab* slimy.
33 *chaudron* insides, guts.
22–34 What new element is now added to the Witches' cauldron?
35 What is the effect of the repetition of these lines?
Song *Black Spirits* another song by the playwright Thomas Middleton.
44 It was believed that a sudden physical pain gave warning of a coming event.

Enter Macbeth

Macbeth
How now, you secret, black, and midnight hags!
What is't you do?

All   A deed without a name.

Macbeth
I conjure you by that which you profess –   50
Howe'er you come to know it – answer me.
Though you untie the winds and let them fight
Against the churches; though the yesty waves
Confound and swallow navigation up;
Though bladed corn be lodg'd and trees blown down;   55
Though castles topple on their warders' heads;
Though palaces and pyramids do slope
Their heads to their foundations; though the treasure
Of nature's germens tumble all together,
Even till destruction sicken – answer me   60
To what I ask you.

First Witch   Speak.

Second Witch   Demand.

Third Witch   We'll answer.

First Witch
Say, if thou'dst rather hear it from our mouths,
Or from our masters?

Macbeth   Call 'em; let me see 'em.

First Witch
Pour in sow's blood that hath eaten
Her nine farrow; grease that's sweaten   65
From the murderer's gibbet throw
Into the flame.

All   Come, high or low;
Thyself and office deftly show.

Thunder. First Apparition, an Armed Head

Macbeth
Tell me, thou unknown power –

First Witch   He knows thy thought.
Hear his speech, but say thou nought.   70

49 *A deed without a name* because it was so dreadful.
50 *I conjure . . . profess* I call upon you in the name of your magical practice.
53 *yesty* yeasty, foaming.
54 *confound* confuse. *navigation* ships.
55 *Though . . . lodg'd* though the unripe corn (bladed) is blown flat.
56 *warders* guards.
57 *pyramids* steeples.
57–58 *slope . . . their foundations* lean over to the ground beneath them.
60 *till destruction sicken* until destruction itself has had enough.
63 *masters* **Who are these?**
63 *Call 'em* **What tone does Macbeth use?**
65 *farrow* piglets. *nine* **What is the significance of the number? What sort of sow must she be?**
sweaten oozed out.
66 *gibbet* gallows.
68 *Thyself . . . show* appear and give your performance as well as you can.
Where on the stage might the apparitions appear from?
Armed Head a helmeted Head. **What significance might this have for Macbeth? The answer may not yet be clear.**

Apparition
Macbeth! Macbeth! Macbeth! Beware Macduff;
Beware the Thane of Fife. Dismiss me. Enough.

He descends

Macbeth
Whate'er thou art, for thy good caution, thanks;
Thou hast harp'd my fear aright. But one word more –
First Witch
He will not be commanded. Here's another,   75
More potent than the first.

Thunder. Second Apparition, a Bloody Child.

Apparition
Macbeth! Macbeth! Macbeth!
Macbeth
Had I three ears, I'd hear thee.
Apparition
Be bloody, bold, and resolute; laugh to scorn
The power of man, for none of woman born   80
Shall harm Macbeth. (*Descends*)
Macbeth
Then live Macduff: what need I fear of thee?
But yet I'll make assurance double sure
And take a bond of fate. Thou shalt not live;
That I may tell pale-hearted fear it lies,   85
And sleep in spite of thunder.

Thunder. Third Apparition, a Child Crowned with a tree in his hand.

What is this
That rises like the issue of a king,
And wears upon his baby brow the round
And top of sovereignty?
All   Listen, but speak not to't.
Apparition
Be lion-mettled, proud, and take no care   90
Who chafes, who frets, or where conspirers are:
Macbeth shall never vanquish'd be until

74 *harp'd . . . aright* you've guessed my real fear correctly.
a Bloody Child **Can you guess its meaning?**
83–84 *I'll make . . . a bond of fate* I'll make absolutely certain by forcing Fate to keep its promise, that is, by killing Macduff.
84 *Thou* Macduff.
85–86 *That . . . thunder* so I can convince myself that my fears are unfounded and I can then begin to sleep despite the thunder. **What do you think Macbeth really means by *thunder*?** Notice how thunder sounds as he speaks.
a Child Crowned with a tree in his hand **What might this mean?**
87 *issue* child.
88–89 *round . . . sovereignty* the king's crown and the height of ambition.
90 *lion-mettled* brave, lionhearted.
90–91 *take care . . . conspirers are* you can ignore those who are angry, who complain and conspire.

Great Birnam Wood to high Dunsinane Hill
Shall come against him. (*Descends*)
Macbeth   That will never be.
Who can impress the forest, bid the tree   95
Unfix his earth-bound root? Sweet bodements! good!
Rebellion's head rise never till the wood
Of Birnam rise, and our high-plac'd Macbeth
Shall live the lease of nature, pay his breath
To time and mortal custom. Yet my heart   100
Throbs to know one thing: tell me, if your art
Can tell so much, shall Banquo's issue ever
Reign in this kingdom?
All   Seek to know no more.
Macbeth
I will be satisfied. Deny me this,
And an eternal curse fall on you! Let me know.   105
Why sinks the cauldron? And what noise is this?

Music of hautboys as the cauldron descends.

First Witch
Show!
Second Witch
Show!
Third Witch
Show!
All
Show his eyes, and grieve his heart;   110
Come like shadows, so depart.

*A Show of eight Kings, the last with a 'crystal' glass in his hand;
Banquo follows.*

Macbeth
Thou art too like the spirit of Banquo; down!
Thy crown does sear mine eye-balls. And thy hair,
Thou other gold-bound brow, is like the first:
A third is like the former. Filthy hags!   115
Why do you show me this? A fourth? Start eyes!
What, will the line stretch out to th'crack of doom?

93 *Great Birnam Wood . . . Hill* these are about twelve miles apart.
94 *That will never be* **What tone does Macbeth now adopt? Why?**
95 *impress* force the tree to become soldiers.
96 *bodements* prophecies.
97 *Rebellion's head* an uprising against him.
98 *Shall live . . . nature* have a normal lease of life.
98–99 *pay . . . custom* that is, die a natural death.
106 *sinks* **where will the cauldron sink?** *noise* music.
hautboys these are oboes.
A Show of eight Kings this would be a mime or dumb show. Such a show was common in plays of the time. The Kings are the eight Stuart Kings of Banquo's line, the last one being James I himself.
113 *sear* burn. *hair* general appearance.
116 *Start, eyes* he would rather they fell out of their sockets than he should see more.
117 *th' crack of doom* a peal of thunder or a trumpet to mark the end of the world.

Another yet? A seventh? I'll see no more.
And yet the eighth appears, who bears a glass
Which shows me many more; and some I see   120
That two-fold balls and treble sceptres carry.
Horrible sight! Now, I see, 'tis true;
For the blood-bolter'd Banquo smiles upon me,
And points at them for his. (*The show vanishes*)
                     What! is this so?

First Witch
Ay, sir, all this is so. But why   125
Stands Macbeth thus amazedly?
Come, sisters, cheer we up his sprites,
And show the best of our delights;
I'll charm the air to give a sound,
While you perform your antic round;   130
That this great king may kindly say,
Our duties did his welcome pay.

        *Music. The **Witches** dance and vanish.*

Macbeth
Where are they? Gone? Let this pernicious hour
Stand aye accursed in the calendar!
Come in, without there.

            *Enter **Lennox***

Lennox   What is your Grace's will?   135
Macbeth
Saw you the Weird Sisters?
Lennox   No, my lord.
Macbeth
Came they not by you?
Lennox   No, indeed my lord.
Macbeth
Infected be the air whereon they ride,
And damn'd all those that trust them! I did hear
The galloping of horse. Who was't came by?   140
Lennox
'Tis two or three, my lord, that bring you word
Macduff is fled to England.

121 *two-fold . . . sceptres* James' double coronation over England and Scotland would be symbolised by the twofold balls. The treble sceptres represent his rule over England, Scotland and Ireland.
123 *blood-bolter'd* his hair matted with blood.
130 *antic round* fantastic dance.
131–132 *this great king . . . pay* these lines could have been addressed to Macbeth. **Could they apply to anyone else? Why?**
139 *And damn'd . . . them* **What point is being made here?**
142 *Macduff . . . England* **How will Macbeth react to this news and why?**

Macbeth	Fled to England!

Lennox

Ay, my good lord.

Macbeth (*aside*)

Time, thou anticipat'st my dread exploits.

The flighty purpose never is o'ertook   145

Unless the deed go with it. From this moment

The very firstlings of my heart shall be

The firstlings of my hand. And even now,

To crown my thoughts with acts, be it thought and done:

The castle of Macduff I will surprise: 150

Seize upon Fife; give to the edge o'th'sword

His wife, his babes, and all unfortunate souls

That trace him in his line. No boasting like a fool;

This deed I'll do before this purpose cool.

But no more sights! – Where are these gentlemen?   155

Come, bring me where they are.

They leave

144 *Time . . . exploits* time has beaten him to it.

145–145 *The flighty . . . it* Macbeth suggests that unless an urgent deed is carried out the moment it is conceived, it will always be too late.

147 *firstlings* first born. In future, Macbeth will act on impulse and emotion, not on reason. **What sort of person behaves like this?**

149 *crown* conclude.

153 *trace* follow.

POINTS TO CONSIDER

? 39–43 Bearing in mind your earlier discussion of Hecate's speech in Act 3 scene 4, how do you react to these lines?

? 51 *Howe'er you come to know it* which of Macbeth's earlier words does this line recall?

? 52–61 What vision of the universe does Macbeth give here? What insight does it give into his own frame of mind?

? 63 Compare Macbeth's willingness to see these spirits with his reaction to Banquo's ghost. What has happened to Macbeth?

? 94–102 How would you describe Macbeth's mood during this speech?

? 101–102 Why does Macbeth still need to ask this question?

? *A Show of eight Kings* How might these Kings be presented on stage? How would James I, when watching the play, react to this episode?

? *Enter Lennox* How does the previous scene affect our view of him? Why do you think he has remained with Macbeth?

ACT FOUR SCENE 1 SUGGESTED ACTIVITIES

Production/Group Work

P1 In groups of three, discuss how you might produce this scene. Pay particular attention to:
- lighting effects
- music
- what form the apparitions would take.

P2 In the same groups, act out lines 1–46 (omitting Hecate). Make a clear distinction between the three Witches in any way you can.

P3 In pairs, consider the changes that have taken place in Macbeth. Think of 5 different words that sum up the sort of man he has become.

Text

T1 a) Re-read lines 4–31 of this scene. Then working in pairs and without the text, fill in the words missing from the speech below. (Write your words in a list on a separate sheet of paper, not in the book.) Try to use Shakespeare's original words if you can remember them. If not, use words that seem appropriate to you.

Round about the cauldron go;
In the _____ entrails throw . . .
Fillet of a fenny _____,
In the cauldron boil and bake;
Eye of newt, and toe of frog,
Wool of bat, and tongue of _____,
Adder's _____ and blind- _____ sting, . . .
Finger of _____ - _____ babe
Ditch-deliver'd by a drab, . . .

b) When you have finished, look at the speech in the text and write down the original words in a list next to your own. Then, with your partner, compare the two lists of words. If you have used different words, discuss with your partner what effect Shakespeare's words convey and how they are different from yours.

c) Working alone and using Shakespeare's original words (from your second list), find a link for each word in the rest of the play.

T2 Add more images to your Image Trees.

Written Work

W1 Re-write the Witches' spells, using your own ingredients but trying as far as possible to keep the same verse.

W1 Imagine that you have been asked to write a front page newspaper report of the events taking place in this scene up to the disappearance of the Witches. Give a headline and write the article.

SCENE 2

Fife. A room in Macduff's castle.
Enter Lady Macduff, her son and Ross.

Lady Macduff
    What had he done to make him fly the land?
Ross
    You must have patience, madam.
Lady Macduff   He had none;
    His flight was madness. When our actions do not,
    Our fears do make us traitors.
Ross   You know not
    Whether it was his wisdom or his fear.   5
Lady Macduff
    Wisdom! To leave his wife, to leave his babes,
    His mansion, and his titles, in a place
    From whence himself does fly? He loves us not;
    He wants the natural touch; for the poor wren,
    The most diminutive of birds, will fight,   10
    Her young.ones in her nest, against the owl.
    All is the fear, and nothing is the love;
    As little is the wisdom, where the flight
    So runs against all reason.
Ross   My dearest coz,
I pray you, school yourself. But, for your husband,   15
He is noble, wise, judicious, and best knows
The fits o'th'season. I dare not speak much further:
But cruel are the times, when we are traitors
And do not know ourselves; when we hold rumour
From what we fear, yet know not what we fear,   20
But float upon a wild and violent sea
Each way and move. I take my leave of you;
Shall not be long but I'll be here again.
Things at the worst will cease, or else climb upward
To what they were before. – My pretty cousin,   25
Blessing upon you!

Fife is the home of Macduff.

3–4 *When our . . traitors* Although Macduff had not committed treachery in the normal sense of the word, fear had made him flee from home and, in Lady Macduff's eyes, this turns him into a traitor.

4–5 What role is Ross adopting here?

9 *wants* lacks; *natural touch* normal instinct to love and protect those dear to you.

9–11 What is the effect of the *owl* and the *wren* in this image?

12–14 *All is . . . reason* fear has taken the place of his love and he seems to have completely lost his reason too since there seems to be no point in his flight.

How does Lady Macduff regard her husband's behaviour?

14 *coz* cousin, though the word was used far more loosely at the time.

15 *school* control; *for* as for.

17 *The fits o'th'season* the changing moods of the time.

18–19 *when we . . . ourselves* when we're considered traitors without even realising it ourselves.

19–20 *When we . . . fear* when we're only too ready to believe rumours because we're so afraid, yet we don't even know what we're afraid of.

22 *Each way and move* tossed in all directions on the waves.

What impression does this image give of the times they're living in?

24 *climb upward* improve.

Lady Macduff
Father'd he is, and yet he's fatherless.

Ross
I am so much a fool, should I stay longer,
It would be my disgrace and your discomfort.
I take my leave at once.

He goes

Lady Macduff   Sirrah, your father's dead: 30
And what will you do now? How will you live?

Son
As birds do, mother.

Lady Macduff   What, with worms and flies?

Son
With what I get, I mean; and so do they.

Lady Macduff
Poor bird! Thou'dst never fear the net nor lime,
The pit-fall nor the gin.   35

Son
Why should I, mother? Poor birds they are not set for.
My father is not dead, for all your saying.

Lady Macduff
Yes, he is dead. How wilt thou do for a father?

Son
Nay, how will you do for a husband?

Lady Macduff
Why, I can buy me twenty at any market.   40

Son
Then you'll buy 'em to sell again.

Lady Macduff
Thou speak'st with all thy wit; and yet i'faith,
With wit enough for thee.

Son
Was my father a traitor, mother?

Lady Macduff
Ay, that he was.   45

Son
What is a traitor?

28–29 What is Ross afraid of?
30 *Sirrah* an affectionate term when used to a child, but contemptuous to a servant.
34 *lime* a sticky substance used to trap birds' feet.
35 *pit-fall* a trap for birds; *gin* a snare.
36 *Poor birds . . . for* no one would set a trap for a bird of little value.
What does this answer suggest about Lady Macduff's son?
41 *Then you'll . . . again* if husbands are so easy to find, then they're not worth having.
42 *wit* sense, intelligence.

Lady Macduff

    Why, one that swears and lies.

Son

    And be all traitors that do so?

Lady Macduff

    Every one that does so is a traitor, and must be hang'd.   50

Son

    And must they all be hang'd that swear and lie?

Lady Macduff

    Every one.

Son

    Who must hang them?

Lady Macduff

    Why, the honest men.

Son

    Then the liars and swearers are fools; for there are   55
    liars and swearers enow to beat the honest men and
    hang up them.

Lady Macduff

    Now, God help thee, poor monkey! But how wilt thou do
    for a father?

Son

    If he were dead, you'd weep for him; if you would   60
    not, it were a good sign that I should quickly have
    a new father.

Lady Macduff

    Poor prattler, how thou talk'st!

Enter a **Messenger**

Messenger

    Bless you, fair dame! I am not to you known,
    Though in your state of honour I am perfect.   65
    I doubt some danger does approach you nearly.
    If you will take a homely man's advice,
    Be not found here; hence, with your little ones.
    To fright you thus, methinks, I am too savage;
    To do worse to you were fell cruelty,   70
    Which is too nigh your person. Heaven preserve you!
    I dare abide no longer.

56 *enow* enough. **What relationship between mother and son is shown here?**

65 *state of honour . . . perfect* I'm well aware of your social standing.

66 *I doubt* I'm afraid.

67 *homely* humble.

69–70 *To fright . . . cruelty* although it is cruel to frighten you in this way, it is less cruel than the danger that threatens you.

How is the tone of the messenger's words different from Ross's?

He goes

Lady Macduff   Whither should I fly?
I have done no harm. But I remember now
I am in this earthly world, where, to do harm
Is often laudable, to do good sometime   75
Accounted dangerous folly; why then, alas,
Do I put up that womanly defence
To say I have done no harm?

Enter **Murderers**

        What are these faces?
First Murderer
    Where is your husband?
Lady Macduff
    I hope, in no such place so unsanctified   80
    Where such as thou mayst find him.
First Murderer   He's a traitor.
Son
    Thou liest, thou shag-hair'd villain.
First Murderer   What, you egg!

stabbing him

    Young fry of treachery!
Son   He has kill'd me, mother.
    Run away, I pray you.

He dies. **Lady Macduff rushes out, crying 'Murder'**

74–76 *where to do . . . folly* a world in which you're praised for doing harm and criticised for doing good. **What tone does Lady Macduff use here?**

80–8 What do these lines suggest are Lady Macduff's real feelings for her husband?

82 *shag-hair'd* with long, shaggy hair.

83 *fry* young fish. **Why are *egg* and *fry* used to describe the Son? What is likely to happen after Lady Macduff rushes off the stage?**

POINTS TO CONSIDER

? 18–19 What has happened to Ross since we last saw him?

? 24–25 *Things . . . before* Has Ross any reason for believing things may improve?

? 74–76 What is Lady Macduff suggesting about life under Macbeth's rule? Where else have we come across a similar set of values?

ACT FOUR SCENE 2 SUGGESTED ACTIVITIES

Production/Group Work

P1 In groups of four, discuss the purpose of this scene. In doing so, consider
a) what would be lost if the scene were omitted?
b) any historical parallel you can think of in which a massacre of innocents takes place.
c) your opinion of Macbeth at this point in the play.

P2 In the same groups, consider Macduff's behaviour and whether or not you feel he is in any way responsible for what has happened.

Text

T1 Add more images to your Image Trees.

T2 Explain how each of your images contributes to the mood of this particular scene.

Written Work

W1 Imagine that Macduff had left a note for his family saying goodbye but without daring to give any clear explanation for going. What might he have written?

W2 What differences in character are there between Lady Macbeth and Lady Macduff? It might help to draw two columns, one for each and write down contrasts next to each other.

SCENE 3

England. Outside King Edward's palace.
Enter Malcolm *and* Macduff.
Malcolm
    Let us seek out some desolate shade, and there
    Weep our sad bosoms empty.
Macduff   Let us rather
    Hold fast the mortal sword, and like good men
    Bestride our down-fall'n birthdom. Each new morn
    New widows howl, new orphans cry; new sorrows

5

The scene now changes to England and the court of Edward the Confessor.
What do we already know of this King?

Strike heaven on the face, that it resounds
As if it felt with Scotland and yell'd out
Like syllable of dolour.

Malcolm   What I believe, I'll wail;
What know, believe; and what I can redress,
As I shall find the time to friend, I will.   10
What you have spoke, it may be so, perchance.
This tyrant, whose sole name blisters our tongues,
Was once thought honest; you have lov'd him well;
He hath not touch'd you yet. I am young, but something
You may deserve of him through me, and wisdom   15
To offer up a weak, poor, innocent lamb
T'appease an angry god.

Macduff
I am not treacherous.

Malcolm   But Macbeth is.
A good and virtuous nature may recoil
In an imperial charge. But I shall crave your pardon;   20
That which you are, my thoughts cannot transpose;
Angels are bright still, though the brightest fell.
Though all things foul would wear the brows of grace,
Yet grace must still look so.

Macduff   I have lost my hopes.

Malcolm
Perchance even there where I did find my doubts.   25
Why in that rawness left you wife and child,
Those precious motives, those strong knots of love,
Without leave-taking? I pray you,
Let not my jealousies be your dishonours,
But my own safeties: you may be rightly just,   30
Whatever I shall think.

Macduff   Bleed, bleed, poor country!
Great tyranny, lay thou thy basis sure,

12 *desolate shade, weep, sad, empty* **What do these words suggest about Malcolm's attitude to Macbeth's kingship in Scotland?**
3 *mortal* fatal.
4 *bestride . . . birthdom* stand over and defend our fatherland in its misfortune as a soldier might protect a fallen comrade.
5–8 *new sorrows . . . dolour* each new grief is like a slap on heaven's face which echoes, as though heaven were in sympathy and giving a similar cry of pain.
2–8 How does Macduff's attitude differ from Malcolm's?
8–10 *What I believe . . . I will* I'll lament only for what I believe to be true and I'll lament only for what I know to be true; anything that I can put right I will, at the appropriate time.
12 What image is used here to describe Macbeth?
14 *He hath not touch'd you yet* **What effect is Shakespeare creating here?**
14–15 *something . . . me* **What does Malcolm fear?**
16, 17, *innocent lamb, angry god* **Which two people are referred to here?**
19–20 *A good . . . charge* even the most virtuous person may fall into evil ways under pressure from a king.
21 *transpose* change. In other words, the way I think about you isn't going to change the way you are.
22 *brightest* Lucifer, the angel who led the rebellion against God.
23 *Though all . . . so* even though Evil attempts to change its appearance and look like Virtue, Virtue remains the same in appearance.
24 *I have lost my hopes* **What do you think Macduff is referring to here?**
25 *there* Macduff's sudden flight to England was to gain Malcolm's help against Macbeth; it is this that has aroused Malcolm's suspicions. **What might Malcolm fear?**
26 *rawness* without protection.
27 *motives* motivations or reasons for action.
29–30 *Let not . . . safeties* don't let my own doubts cast a slight on your honour, but let them be seen simply as a way of protecting myself.
32 *basis* foundation.
32–33 *Great tyranny . . . check thee* The effect of Malcolm's suspicions is for Macduff to despair of ever being able to overcome Macbeth. He sees Macbeth here as being allowed to rule as a tyrant completely unchecked. **What tone will Macduff use here?**

For goodness dare not check thee! Wear thou thy wrongs,
The title is affeer'd. Fare thee well, lord.
I would not be the villain that thou think'st   35
For the whole space that's in the tyrant's grasp
And the rich East to boot.

Malcolm   Be not offended:
I speak not as in absolute fear of you.
I think our country sinks beneath the yoke;
It weeps, it bleeds; and each new day a gash   40
Is added to her wounds. I think withal
There would be hands uplifted in my right;
And here, from gracious England, have I offer
Of goodly thousands. But, for all this,
When I shall tread upon the tyrant's head,   45
Or wear it on my sword, yet my poor country
Shall have more vices than it had before;
More suffer, and more sundry ways than ever,
By him that shall succeed.

Macduff   What should he be?

Malcolm
It is myself I mean; in whom I know   50
All the particulars of vice so grafted,
That, when they shall be open'd, black Macbeth
Will seem as pure as snow, and the poor state
Esteem him as a lamb, being compar'd
With my confineless harms.

Macduff   Not in the legions   55
Of horrid hell can come a devil more damn'd
In evils to top Macbeth.

Malcolm   I grant him bloody,
Luxurious, avaricious, false, deceitful,
Sudden, malicious, smacking of every sin
That has a name; but there's no bottom, none,   60
In my voluptuousness. Your wives, your daughters,
Your matrons, and your maids, could not fill up
The cistern of my lust; and my desire
All continent impediments would o'erbear
That did oppose my will. Better Macbeth   65
Than such an one to reign.

33–34 *Wear . . . affeer'd* Macbeth can continue his life of crime. Since Malcolm will not oppose his title (of king), the title is now confirmed.

37 *East* regarded as the source of wealth. *to boot* as well.

39 *sinks beneath the yoke* **What image is used in this comparison?**

40–41 A new image is introduced here to describe the condition of Scotland under Macbeth's rule. It is an image that will recur during the remaining scenes of the play. **What is the image and do you think it is an appropriate one?**

41 *withal* also, moreover.

42 I would find support.

43 *gracious England* Edward the Confessor, a man who had found grace with God.

48–49 *More suffer . . . succeed* Malcolm suggests that Scotland will suffer a great deal more and in many different ways under the rule of the next King, that is, himself. **What is he suggesting about himself?**

51 *particulars* species, different varieties.

51 *grafted* implanted. **What comparison is being made through the image of grafting?**

52 *open'd* **Bearing in mind the previous image, what is being suggested through the word** *open'd***?**

55 *confineless harms* unlimited evil.

57 *top* outdo, surpass.

58 *luxurious* full of lust. The word has only recently changed to its present-day meaning. *avaricious* mean, miserly.

59 *sudden* violent. *smacking* with a taste of.

61 *voluptuousness* lustfulness.

60–63 *bottom, fill up, cistern* **What image is used here?**

63–65 *my desire . . . my will* my desire or lust would overcome everything that tried to restrain me.

Macduff　　　　　　　　Boundless intemperance
In nature is a tyranny; it hath been
Th'untimely emptying of the happy throne
And fall of many kings. But fear not yet
To take upon you what is yours. You may　　　　　70
Convey your pleasures in a spacious plenty,
And yet seem cold, the time you may so hoodwink.
We have willing dames enough; there cannot be
That vulture in you to devour so many
As will to greatness dedicate themselves,　　　　75
Finding it so inclin'd.
Malcolm　　　　　　　With this there grows
In my most ill-compos'd affection such
A staunchless avarice, that, were I King,
I should cut off the nobles for their lands,
Desire his jewels, and this other's house;　　　　80
And my more-having would be as a sauce
To make me hunger more, that I should forge
Quarrels unjust against the good and loyal,
Destroying them for wealth.
Macduff　　　　　　　　This avarice
Sticks deeper, grows with more pernicious root　　85
Than summer-seeming lust; and it hath been
The sword of our slain kings: yet do not fear;
Scotland hath foisons to fill up your will,
Of your mere own. All these are portable,
With other graces weigh'd.　　　　　　　90
Malcolm
But I have none; the king-becoming graces,
As justice, verity, temp'rance, stableness,
Bounty, perseverance, mercy, lowliness,
Devotion, patience, courage, fortitude –
I have no relish of them; but abound　　　　　95
In the division of each several crime,
Acting it many ways. Nay, had I power, I should
Pour the sweet milk of concord into hell,
Uproar the universal peace, confound
All unity on earth.
Macduff　　　　　O Scotland! Scotland!　　　100

66–67 *Boundless intemperance . . . tyranny* complete lack of selfcontrol takes over a man's nature like a tyrant.

70–72 *You may . . . hoodwink* you may obtain your pleasures in secret and still, by deceiving everyone, keep your virtuous reputation intact.

73–76 *there cannot . . . so inclin'd* your appetite can't be so large that it won't be satisfied by the number of women who would be prepared to give themselves to you as a king. **What impression of himself is Malcolm trying to create here? How is he likely to feel about this reply from Macduff?**

77 *ill-compos'd affection* a nature composed of ill assorted vices.

78 *staunchless* insatiable.

79 *cut off* kill.

82 *forge* make up.

85 *sticks deeper* is more deeply rooted.

86 *summer-seeming* lust will pass with time, like the seasons.

88 *foisons* rich supplies.

89 *Of your mere own* of what really belongs to you.

89 *portable* bearable.

92 *verity* truthfulness.

95 *relish* trace.

96 *In the division . . . crime* the variations of every possible form of sin.

Malcolm

    If such a one be fit to govern, speak:
    I am as I have spoken.

Macuff   Fit to govern!

    No, not to live! O nation miserable,
    With an untitled tyrant bloody-scept'red,
    When shalt thou see thy wholesome days again,   105
    Since that the truest issue of thy throne
    By his own interdiction stands accus'd
    And does blaspheme his breed? Thy royal father
    Was a most sainted king; the queen that bore thee,
    Oft'ner upon her knees than on her feet,   110
    Died every day she liv'd. Fare thee well!
    These evils thou repeat'st upon thyself
    Hath banish'd me from Scotland. O my breast,
    Thy hope ends here!

Malcolm   Macduff, this noble passion,

    Child of integrity, hath from my soul   115
    Wip'd the black scruples, reconcil'd my thoughts
    To thy good truth and honour. Devilish Macbeth
    By many of these trains hath sought to win me
    Into his power, and modest wisdom plucks me
    From over-credulous haste. But God above   120
    Deal between thee and me; for even now
    I put myself to thy direction, and
    Unspeak mine own detraction, here abjure
    The taints and blames I laid upon myself
    For strangers to my nature. I am yet   125
    Unknown to woman; never forsworn;
    Scarcely have coveted what was mine own;
    At no time broke my faith; would not betray
    The devil to his fellow; and delight
    No less in truth than life. My first false speaking   130
    Was this upon myself. What I am truly
    Is thine and my poor country's to command:
    Whither indeed, before thy here-approach,
    Old Siward, with ten thousand warlike men
    Already at a point, was setting forth.   135
    Now we'll together, and the chance of goodness

104 *untitled* not entitled to be king.

104 *bloody-sceptred* **Why?**

107 *interdiction* self-accusation.

108 *blaspheme his breed* slander and therefore bring disgrace on his family.

111 *Died . . . liv'd* led a devout and penitent life as though each day were her last.

111–113 *Fare thee well . . . Scotland* these vices you possess are the very ones that made me leave Scotland.

115 *Child of integrity* brought about by your honesty.

116 *scruples* suspicions, doubts.

118 *trains* plots, schemes.

119–120 *modest wisdom . . . haste* caution stops me from believing too readily.

123 *Unspeak mine own detraction* I withdraw all my earlier accusations against myself.

123 *abjure* deny.

125 *For strangers* as foreign.

135 *at a point* ready for action.

136–137 *the chance . . . quarrel* I hope our chances of success are equal to the justice of our cause.

Be like our warranted quarrel. Why are you silent?

Macduff

Such welcome and unwelcome things at once
'Tis hard to reconcile.

Enter a **Doctor**

Malcolm

Well, more anon. Comes the King forth, I pray you?   140

Doctor

Ay sir. There are a crew of wretched souls
That stay his cure. Their malady convinces
The great assay of art; but at his touch,
Such sanctity hath heaven given his hand,
They presently amend.

Malcolm   I thank you, doctor.   145

The **Doctor** *leaves.*

Macduff

What's the disease he means?

Malcolm   'Tis called the evil:
A most miraculous work in this good king,
Which often, since my here-remain in England,
I have seen him do. How he solicits heaven,
Himself best knows; but strangely-visited people,   150
All swoln and ulcerous, pitiful to the eye,
The mere despair of surgery, he cures,
Hanging a golden stamp about their necks,
Put on with holy prayers; and 'tis spoken,
To the succeeding royalty he leaves   155
The healing benediction. With this strange virtue,
He hath a heavenly gift of prophecy;
And sundry blessings hang about his throne,
That speak him full of grace.

Enter **Ross**

Macduff   See, who comes here?

Malcolm

My countryman; but yet I know him not.   160

Macduff
My ever gentle cousin, welcome hither.
Malcolm
I know him now. Good God, betimes remove
The means that makes us strangers!
Ross   Sir, amen.
Macduff
Stands Scotland where it did?
Ross   Alas, poor country!
Almost afraid to know itself. It cannot   165
Be call'd our mother, but our grave; where nothing,
But who knows nothing, is once seen to smile;
Where sighs, and groans, and shrieks, that rent the air,
Are made, not mark'd; where violent sorrow seems
A modern ecstasy; the dead man's knell   170
Is there scarce ask'd for who; and good men's lives
Expire before the flowers in their caps,
Dying or ere they sicken.
Macduff   O, relation
Too nice, and yet too true!
Malcolm   What's the newest grief?
Ross
That of an hour's age doth hiss the speaker;   175
Each minute teems a new one.
Macduff   How does my wife?
Ross
Why, well.
Macduff   And all my children?
Ross   Well too.
Macduff
The tyrant has not batter'd at their peace?
Ross
No; they were well at peace when I did leave 'em.
Macduff
Be not niggard of your speech: how goes't?   180
Ross
When I came hither to transport the tidings,
Which I have heavily borne, there ran a rumour

162 *betimes* quickly.

163 *The means* **What are these?**

164 *Stands . . . did* are things the same as when I left?

166–167 *where nothing . . . smile* where the only people who smile are those who don't know what's going on.

168 *rent* rend, tear apart.

169 *Are made, not mark'd* sighs, groans, and shrieks pass by unnoticed because they are heard so often.

170 *modern ecstasy* a rather ordinary, familiar emotion.

170–171 *the dead man's . . . for who* no one bothers to ask who has died when the bell tolls.

173 *Dying . . . sicken* men die before they are even ill. **Why? What picture of Scotland is the audience given here?**

174 *Too nice . . . true* too detailed and yet only too true.

174 *newest* latest. **How will this question affect Ross?**

175 *That . . . speaker* news only one hour old is already out of date and is therefore hissed at.

176 *teems* brings forth.

177 *why, well* **What does Ross really mean here? Why does he answer in this way?**

178 *The tyrant . . . peace?* **What insight into Macduff does this question give?**

180 *niggard of your speech* reluctant to say very much. **What does *niggard* suggest about Ross's manner?**

181–182 *the tidings . . . heavily borne* **What is Ross perhaps trying to do here?**

Of many worthy fellows that were out;
Which was to my belief witness'd the rather
For that I saw the tyrant's power afoot.   185
Now is the time of help; your eye in Scotland
Would create soldiers, make our women fight,
To doff their dire distresses.

Malcolm   Be't their comfort
We are coming thither. Gracious England hath
Lent us good Siward and ten thousand men –   190
An older and a better soldier none
That Christendom gives out.

Ross   Would I could answer
This comfort with the like! But I have words
That would be howl'd out in the desert air,
Where hearing should not latch them.

Macduff   What concern they?   195
The general cause? Or is it a fee-grief
Due to some single breast?

Ross   No mind that's honest
But in it shares some woe, though the main part
Pertains to you alone.

Macduff   If it be mine,
Keep it not from me; quickly let me have it.   200

Ross
Let not your ears despise my tongue for ever,
Which shall possess them with the heaviest sound
That ever yet they heard.

Macduff   Hum! I guess at it.

Ross
Your castle is surpris'd; your wife and babes
Savagely slaughter'd. To relate the manner,   205
Were, on the quarry of these murder'd deer,
To add the death of you.

Malcolm   Merciful heaven!
What, man! Ne'er pull your hat upon your brows;
Give sorrow words. The grief that does not speak
Whispers the o'er-fraught heart and bids it break.   210

Macduff
My children too?

183 *were out* out fighting against Macbeth.

184 *witness'd* proved.

185 *the tyrant's power afoot* Macbeth's army on the march. **What, therefore, is the rumour Ross has heard?**

186 *Your eye* your presence.

188 *To doff . . . distresses* to cast off their troubles (like clothes).

195 *Latch* catch. *Where hearing . . . them* where they won't be heard.

196–197 *a fee-grief . . . breast* grief affecting just one person.

197 *honest* honourable.

202 *possess* inform.

203 *Hum! I guess at it.* **How would Macduff say these words?**

204 *surpris'd* seized.

205–207 *To relate . . . death of you* if I told you how they were killed, it would be the death of you. *quarry* slaughtered animals.

208 *Ne'er pull . . . brows* **What is Macduff doing at this moment and why?**

210 *Whispers . . . heart* whispers to the overburdened heart.
Malcolm suggests that unless Macduff openly shares his grief, his heart will break.

Ross   Wife, children, servants, all
That could be found.
Macduff   And I must be from thence!
My wife kill'd too?
Ross   I have said.
Malcolm   Be comforted.
Let's make us med'cines of our great revenge,
To cure this deadly grief.   215
Macduff
He has no children. All my pretty ones?
Did you say all? O hell-kite! All?
What, all my pretty chickens and their dam
At one fell swoop?
Malcolm
Dispute it like a man.
Macduff   I shall do so;   220
But I must also feel it as a man.
I cannot but remember such things were
That were most precious to me. Did heaven look on,
And would not take their part? Sinful Macduff!
They were all struck for thee – naught that I am;   225
Not for their own demerits, but for mine,
Fell slaughter on their souls. Heaven rest them now!
Malcolm
Be this the whetstone of your sword: let grief
Convert to anger; blunt not the heart, enrage it.
Macduff
O, I could play the woman with mine eyes   230
And braggart with my tongue! But, gentle heavens,
Cut short all intermission; front to front
Bring thou this fiend of Scotland and myself;
Within my sword's length set him; if he scape,
Heaven forgive him too!
Malcolm   This tune goes manly.   235
Come, go we to the King. Our power is ready;
Our lack is nothing but our leave. Macbeth
Is ripe for shaking, and the pow'rs above
Put on their instruments. Receive what cheer you may;

212 *And I must . . . thence* and I had to be away at that time! **What tone does Macduff use here?**

214–215 *Let's make us medicines . . . grief* **What image recurs here to describe Scotland's condition?**

216 *He has no children* **Who does *he* refer to?**

217 *hell-kite* a bird that swoops down and kills other birds. **Who is Macduff referring to?**

218 *dam* mother.

220 *Dispute it* fight it.

222 *things* **What does Macduff mean here?**

225 *naught* worthless.

226 *demerits* faults.

228 *whetstone* stone for sharpening knives. **What is Malcolm suggesting through this image?**

229 *convert* change. *blunt . . . it* don't control your feelings, show them passionately.

230 *play . . . eyes* weep.

231 *braggart . . . tongue* boasting (of revenge).

232 *intermission* delay.

234–235 *if he 'scape . . . him too* he is as likely to escape as it is likely that both Heaven and I will forgive him. In other words, Macduff is now fully resolved to take his revenge on Macbeth.

235 *manly* properly.

237 *Our lack . . . leave* all that's missing now is for us to say goodbye.

238 *ripe for shaking* **What image does Malcolm use here to describe Macbeth? Is it appropriate?**

238–239 *the pow'rs above . . . instruments* Malcolm sees himself and Macduff as instruments of good working for God.

239 *cheer* comfort.

The night is long that never finds the day.   240

They leave

POINTS TO CONSIDER

? 25–31 How will Macduff feel after this speech? How will the events of the previous scene affect the audience's reaction both to Macduff and to Malcolm?

? 44–66 How do you think Macduff feels at this moment? How might an actor playing his part show these feelings?

? 70–72 Where else in the play has the idea of adopting a deceptive appearance been suggested?

? 98, 99 *concord into hell, uproar . . . peace, confound all unity* – where have we heard such talk before?

? 120 *God above* There are many religious references in the remaining scenes of the play. What purpose do they serve?

? 179 *well at peace* How do you respond to Ross's use of a pun at this moment?

? 186–188 Why do you think Ross is asking for Malcolm and Macduff's help before telling them the bad news?

? 205–207 What effect is created by using the image of a deer? Ross has left *the manner* of Lady Macduff's death to Macduff's imagination. Is it better this way?

? 217 *hell-kite* How is this description appropriate?

? 200–235 What different emotions does Macduff experience at hearing the news of his family's massacre?

? 238–239 Where in the play have we seen people used as the instruments of evil working for the Devil?

? 240 Which earlier line in the play does this echo?

ACT FOUR SCENE 3 SUGGESTED ACTIVITIES

Production/Group Work

P1 In groups of four, discuss whether or not you feel that Malcolm is justified in testing Macduff in the way he does so here. Consider also the following questions:
- Can you think of any other way he might have used to find out whether or not Macduff was a traitor?
- What further information does this scene provide about Malcolm's character?
- How do you think Macduff's attitude to Malcolm might change after this episode?
- What point about human behaviour (made frequently in other parts of the play) is Shakespeare making in this scene?

P2 Ross has to break the bad news to Macduff. Would you criticise him at all for the way he does so? In groups of three, discuss this and then re-enact a similar situation (but make up your own details) in which one person breaks bad news to the others.

Text

T1 a) Re-read lines 146–159. Then working in pairs but without the text, fill in the words missing from the speech below. (Write your words in a list on a separate sheet of paper, not in the book.) Try to use Shakespeare's original words if you can remember them. If not, use words that seem appropriate to you.

'Tis called the evil:
A most _____ work in this _____ king,
Which often, since my here-remain in _____,
I have seen him do. How he solicits _____,
Himself best knows; but _____-_____people,
All swoln and ulcerous, _____ to the eye,
The mere despair of surgery, he _____,
Hanging a _____ stamp about their necks,
Put on with _____ _____; and 'tis spoken,
To the _____ royalty he leaves
The _____ _____. With this strange _____,
He hath a _____ gift of prophecy;
And sundry _____ hang about his throne,
That speak him full of _____.

b) When you have finished, look at the speech in the text and write down the original words in a list next to your own. Then, with your partner, compare the two lists of words. If you have used different words, discuss with your partner what effect Shakespeare's words convey and how they are different from yours.

c) Working on your own and using Shakespeare's original words (from your second list), consider what these words suggest about Edward the Confessor. Write two or three sentences drawing a contrast between Macbeth as a king and Edward.

T2 Add more images to your Image Trees.

Written Work

W1 In line 13, Malcolm says of Macbeth that he 'was once thought honest'. In a single paragraph, give a thumbnail sketch of Macbeth through the eyes of young Malcolm as he might have been before the action of the play began. Concentrate only on Macbeth's strengths and give your sketch a context, (for example, a meeting between Macbeth and Malcolm in Duncan's palace).

W2 This scene is sometimes omitted from productions of the play. Draw two columns, one labelled *Advantages* and the other *Disadvantages* and fill in notes in each to indicate what would be gained and what would be lost by omitting the scene.

Act Five

<u>SCENE 1</u>

Dunsinane. A room in Macbeth's castle.
Enter a **Doctor of Physic** *and a* **Waiting Gentle-woman**

Doctor
    I have two nights watch'd with you, but can perceive
    no truth in your report. When was it she last
    walk'd?

Gentle-woman
    Since his Majesty went into the field, I have seen
    her rise from her bed, throw her nightgown upon   5
    her, unlock her closet, take forth paper, fold it,
    write upon't, read it, afterwards seal it, and again
    return to bed; yet all this while in a most
    fast sleep.

Doctor
    A great perturbation in nature, to receive at   10
    once the benefit of sleep and do the effects of
    watching! In this slumbry agitation, besides her
    walking and other actual performances what, at any
    time, have you heard her say?

Gentle-woman
    That, sir, which I will not report after her.   15

Doctor
    You may to me; and 'tis most meet you should.

Gentle-woman
    Neither to you nor to any one, having no witness to
    confirm my speech.

The scene takes place in Macbeth's castle in Scotland.
Notice that the Doctor, the Gentlewoman and Lady Macbeth all speak in prose, not verse. (see notes on Shakespeare's style). **As you look closely at the scene, consider why Shakespeare made this change.**

1 *watch'd* stayed up
4 *into the field* into battle (against the rebels)
5 *nightgown* dressing gown
6 *closet* writing box
10–12 *A great perturbation....watching!* it is a very disturbed nature that causes her to sleep and yet to behave as though she were awake.
16 *meet* proper
17–18 What do you think the Gentlewoman has heard? What reasons might she have for not repeating to the Doctor what she has overheard Lady Macbeth saying?

Enter **Lady Macbeth,** *with a taper*

Lo you! here she comes. This is her very guise; and, upon my life, fast asleep. Observe her; stand close.

Doctor

How came she by that light?

Gentle-woman

Why, it stood by her: she has light by her continually; 'tis her command.

Doctor

You see her eyes are open.

Gentle-woman

Ay, but their sense is shut.

Doctor

What is it she does now? Look how she rubs her hands.

Gentle-woman

It is an accustomed action with her, to seem thus washing her hands; I have known her continue in this a quarter of an hour.

Lady Macbeth

Yet here's a spot.

Doctor

Hark! she speaks. I will set down what comes from her to satisfy my remembrance the more strongly.

Lady Macbeth

Out, damned spot! Out, I say! One, two; why then 'tis time to do't. Hell is murky! Fie, my lord, fie! a soldier and afeard? What need we fear who knows it, when none can call our pow'r to account? Yet who would have thought the old man to have had so much blood in him?

Doctor

Do you mark that?

19 *guise* her usual appearance
21 *close* hidden
23–24 Lady Macbeth cannot now endure darkness.
27–28 Here Lady Macbeth puts down the taper and goes through the motions of washing her hands over and over again. **Why do you think this happens?**
32 *yet* still, *a spot* of blood
34 *satisfy....strongly* to help me remember more clearly later.
35 *One, two* **What does this refer to?**
42 What is the effect of Lady Macbeth's use of rhyme in this line?

Doctor
Go to, go to; you have known what you should not.
Gentle-woman
She has spoke what she should not, I am sure of
that. Heaven knows what she has known.
Lady-Macbeth
Here's the smell of the blood still: all the
perfumes of Arabia will not sweeten this   50
little hand. Oh! oh! oh!
Doctor
What a sigh is there! The heart is sorely charg'd.
Gentle-woman
I would not have such a heart in my bosom for the
dignity of the whole body.
Doctor
Well, well, well.   55
Gentle-woman
Pray God it be, sir.
Doctor
This disease is beyond my practice: yet I have known
those which have walk'd in their sleep who have died
holily in their beds.
Lady Macbeth
Wash your hands, put on your nightgown; look not   60
so pale. I tell you again, Banquo's buried; he
cannot come out on's grave.
Doctor
Even so?
Lady Macbeth
To bed, to bed; there's knocking at the gate. Come
come, come, come, give me your hand. What's   65
done cannot be undone. To bed, to bed, to bed.

She goes

Doctor
Foul whisp'rings are abroad. Unnatural deeds
Do breed unnatural troubles; infected minds
To their deaf pillows will discharge their secrets.

46 *Go to* Our modern equivalent might be a clicking of the tongue to express disapproval.
52 *sorely charged* deeply, heavily burdened.
54 *dignity of the whole body* The Gentlewoman would not be prepared to take on Lady Macbeth's suffering, even in exchange for being queen.
57 *my practice* my medical expertise.
62 *out on's* out of his.
67 *Foul...abroad* people are spreading evil rumours around.
68 *breed* lead to. *infected minds* **What impression of Scotland does Shakespeare give by repeating this image of disease?**

More needs she the divine than the physician.　　　70
God, God forgive us all! Look after her;
Remove from her the means of all annoyance,
And still keep eyes upon her. So, good night.
My mind she has mated, and amaz'd my sight.
I think, but dare not speak.　　　　　　　　75
Gentle-woman　　　　　Good night, good doctor.

They leave

70 *divine* priest.
72 *means of annoyance* means of injuring herself. **What does the Doctor fear?**
73 *still* always.
74 *mated* confused, bewildered.
75 *I dare not speak* **Why not?**

POINTS TO CONSIDER

? Setting. A Doctor is present. How does this provide a link with the images of the previous scene?

? 17–18 What impression do we gain here of the character of the Gentlewoman?

? 23–24 Why do you think Lady Macbeth needs light? What associations have darkness had for her?

? 35–40 These are important lines for understanding Lady Macbeth's present state of mind. How would you describe it? Which earlier incidents is she now recalling?

? 43–45 *No more...starting* Which moment earlier in the play does this recall?

? 75 What impression of Scotland are we left with at this moment?

ACT FIVE SCENE 1 SUGGESTED ACTIVITIES

Production/Group Work

P1 'Enter Lady Macbeth with a taper'. This is the first time we have seen Lady Macbeth since the middle of Act Three. In groups of three, discuss how, as producer of the play, you are going to indicate by Lady Macbeth's appearance and manner the changes that have taken place in her. Then, in the same groups, mime the scene.

P2 This is also the last time we see Lady Macbeth on stage. In larger groups of about six, discuss the following questions:
- What are your feelings towards Lady Macbeth now?
- Do you think that she has got what she deserves?
- Do you feel sorry for her?
- As producer of the play, how could you manipulate the reactions of your audience towards her or against her?

Text

T1 Below are a series of statements spoken by or about Lady Macbeth. All these are made **ironic** because of what has gone before. (See notes on Shakespeare's style, p 150.) For each quotation given, find the earlier reference which creates the ironic effect. When you have found your quotations, work with a partner and compare the lines you have chosen.
- a) she has light by her continually;
  'tis her command. (lines 23,24)
- b) Yet here's a spot (line 32)
- c) Hell is murky (line 36)
- d) Yet who would have thought the old man to have had so much blood in him? (lines 39–40)
- e) Find an earlier parallel statement to the following:
  All the perfumes of Arabia will not sweeten this little hand.

(lines 49–50)

T2 Discuss with your partner **a)** why Shakespeare has chosen prose for most of this scene and **b)** why the last nine lines are written in verse.

T3 Add more images to your Image Trees.

Written Work

W1 The Gentlewoman describes the way Lady Macbeth in her sleepwalking takes out paper and writes on it. Write down for yourself what you imagine Lady Macbeth might have written.

W2 Make up your own 'patient's notes' as the Doctor might have written them for his patient, Lady Macbeth. Then write them as a present-day doctor might have done.

SCENE 2

The country near Dunsinane. Drum and colours.
Enter **Menteith, Caithness, Angus, Lennox** *and* **Soldiers**

Menteith
The English power is near, led on by Malcolm,
His uncle Siward, and the good Macduff.
Revenges burn in them; for their dear causes
Would to the bleeding and the grim alarm
Excite the mortified man.
Angus   Near Birnam wood   5
Shall we well meet them; that way are they coming.
Caithness
Who knows if Donalbain be with his brother?
Lennox
For certain, sir, he is not. I have a file
Of all the gentry: there is Siward's son,
And many unrough youths that even now   10
Protest their first of manhood.
Menteith   What does the tyrant?
Caithness
Great Dunsinane he strongly fortifies.
Some say he's mad; others, that lesser hate him,
Do call it valiant fury; but, for certain,
He cannot buckle his distemper'd cause   15
Within the belt of rule.
Angus   Now does he feel
His secret murders sticking on his hands;
Now minutely revolts upbraid his faith-breach;
Those he commands move only in command,
Nothing in love. Now does he feel his title
Hang loose about him, like a giant's robe   20
Upon a dwarfish thief.
Menteith   Who then shall blame
His pester'd senses to recoil and start,
When all that is within him does condemn
Itself for being there?

The scene moves outside to the countryside near Macbeth's castle where a number of his former supporters now gather together to fight against him.

Drum and colours the army arrives to the sound of the drum and carrying the banners of their regiment.

1 *power* army.
3–5 *for their . . . man* for the causes close to their hearts are so powerful that they would stir up even a dead man (mortified) to answer the call to fight.
5 *Birnam wood* **How does this reference alert the audience?**
6 *well* likely.
7 *file* list.
10 *unrough* not yet having shaved.
11 *Protest . . . manhood* insist on proving their manhood by fighting.
15–16 *He cannot buckle . . . rule* he cannot control his rebellious men just as a man with a large paunch cannot hold in his waist with a belt.
17 *sticking on his hands* like the blood after Duncan's murder.
18 *Now minutely . . . faith-breach* every minute another man deserts him in condemnation of his own treachery.
19–20 *Those . . . love* those who obey him only do so out of duty, not because they love him.
22–25 *Who then . . . there* who can blame his troubled nerves for their violent reaction when all his faculties rebel against his whole being for belonging to him. **What state of mind does this suggest in Macbeth?**

Caithness   Well, march we on,   25
To give obedience where 'tis truly ow'd.
Meet we the med'cine of the sickly weal,
And with him pour we in our country's purge,
Each drop of us.
Lennox   Or so much as it needs
To dew the sovereign flower and drown the weeds.   30
Make we our march towards Birnam.

They all march off.

27 *med'cine* the doctor, here Malcolm. *weal* state.
This echoes another earlier image. **Which one?**
28–29 *And with him . . . drop of us* let us together shed all our blood to cure our country of its disease. Blood-letting, that is, drawing off blood from the patient, was an important treatment for illness at the time.
30 *To dew* to water. **What is meant by the *sovereign flower* and the *weeds*?**

SCENE 3

Dunsinane. A room in Macbeth's castle.
Enter **Macbeth, Doctor** *and* **Attendants**

Macbeth
Bring me no more reports; let them fly all:
Till Birnam wood remove to Dunsinane
I cannot taint with fear. What's the boy Malcolm?
Was he not born of woman? The spirits that know
All mortal consequences have pronounc'd me thus: 5
'Fear not Macbeth; no man that's born of woman
Shall e'er have power upon thee'. Then fly, false thanes,
And mingle with the English epicures.
The mind I sway by and the heart I bear
Shall never sag with doubt nor shake with fear.   10

Enter **Servant**

The devil damn thee black, thou cream-fac'd loon!
Where got'st thou that goose look?
Servant
There is ten thousand –
Macbeth   Geese, villain?
Servant   Soldiers, sir.

The scene switches back to the castle and we see Macbeth again after some time.

1 *let them fly all* what do I care if all my thanes leave me?
2 Macbeth is clinging on to the Witches' prophecy. **What does the audience know of Birnam wood at this moment?**
3 *taint with fear* grow weak with fear. *boy Malcolm* **What is the effect of this phrase and why does Macbeth use it?**
4 *spirits* the Witches.
5 *mortal consequences* the course of human events.
8 *epicures* given to easy or soft living. The English were regarded as such in contrast with the hardy Scots.
9 *sway by* rule myself with.
11 *loon* rogue, fool.
12 *goose look* silly expression. Geese are meant to be particularly silly creatures.

Macbeth

    Go, prick thy face, and over-red thy fear,
    Thou lily-liver'd boy. What soldiers, patch?   15
    Death of thy soul! Those linen cheeks of thine
    Are counsellors to fear. What soldiers, whey-face?

Servant

    The English force, so please you.

Macbeth

    Take thy face hence.

The **Servant** *leaves.*

    Seyton! – I am sick at heart,
    When I behold – Seyton, I say! – This push   20
    Will cheer me ever, or disseat me now.
    I have liv'd long enough. My way of life
    Is fall'n into the sear, the yellow leaf;
    And that which should accompany old age,
    As honour, love, obedience, troops of friends,   25
    I must not look to have; but, in their stead,
    Curses not loud but deep, mouth-honour, breath,
    Which the poor heart would fain deny, and dare not.
    Seyton!

Enter **Seyton**

Seyton

    What's your gracious pleasure?

Macbeth   What news more?   30

Seyton

    All is confirm'd, my lord, which was reported.

Macbeth

    I'll fight till from my bones my flesh be hack'd.
    Give me my armour.

Seyton   'Tis not needed yet.

Macbeth

    I'll put it on.
    Send out more horses, skirr the country round;   35
    Hang those that talk of fear. Give me mine armour.
    How does your patient, doctor?

14 *Go . . . fear* go and prick your face to colour your white skin red.

15 *lily-liver'd* cowardly. *patch* fool, clown.

16 *linen* pure white.

17 *counsellors to fear* excite fear in other people. *whey-face* a face the colour of thin, skimmed milk.

19 *Seyton* the armourbearer of the king.

20 *When I behold* **What was Macbeth then going to say?**

20–21 *This push . . . now* this attack from the English will either confirm my position on the throne (and leave me happy) or take the throne from me immediately.

23 *sear . . . leaf* the withered state, the autumn of life when leaves turn yellow.

27 *mouth-honour* lip service, that is, words spoken but not necessarily meant.

28 *Which . . . dare not* which the fearful speaker (like the Servant) would rather not say at all, but dare not.

31 *All is confirm'd* **What does this refer to? Why does Seyton only refer indirectly to the news?**

35 *skirr* scour.

35–36 What tone of voice does Macbeth use here?

Doctor   Not so sick, my lord,
　　As she is troubled with thick-coming fancies
　　That keep her from her rest.
Macbeth   Cure her of that:
　　Canst thou not minister to a mind diseas'd,   40
　　Pluck from the memory a rooted sorrow,
　　Raze out the written troubles of the brain,
　　And with some sweet oblivious antidote
　　Cleanse the stuff'd bosom of that perilous stuff
　　Which weighs upon the heart?
Doctor   Therein the patient   45
　　Must minister to himself.
Macbeth
　　Throw physic to the dogs – I'll none of it.
　　Come, put mine armour on; give me my staff.
　　Seyton, send out. Doctor, the thanes fly from me.
　　Come, sir, dispatch. If thou couldst, doctor, cast   50
　　The water of my land, find her disease,
　　And purge it to a sound and pristine health,
　　I would applaud thee to the very echo,
　　That should applaud again. – Pull't off, I say. –
　　What rhubarb, senna, or what purgative drug,   55
　　Would scour these English hence? Hear'st thou of them?
Doctor
　　Ay, my good lord; your royal preparation
　　Makes us hear something.
Macbeth   Bring it after me.
　　I will not be afraid of death and bane
　　Till Birnam forest come to Dunsinane.   60

　　　　　　　　All but the **Doctor** *leave.*

Doctor
　　Were I from Dunsinane away and clear,
　　Profit again should hardly draw me here.

　　　　　　　　He goes

38 *thick-coming fancies* hallucinations crowding in on her thick and fast.
40 *minister to* treat and cure.
42 *Raze out* erase. *written . . . brain* trouble deeply imprinted in the brain.
43 *oblivious antidote* medicine to make one forget.
44 *stuff'd* overburdened.
What assumptions does Macbeth make about the Doctor's skills?
47 *physic* the skill of the doctor.
50 *dispatch* hurry.
50–51 *cast the water . . . disease* diagnose the illness by examining the urine.
52 *pristine* original, such as it was before.
53–54 *I would applaud . . . again* my applause would be so loud that it would echo and then re-echo.
54 *Pull't off I say* **Why do you think Macbeth now asks Seyton to take off his armour?**
55 *rhubarb, senna* These are laxatives which would purge the body. **In what terms, therefore does Macbeth see the English?**
58 *it* the armour.
59 *bane* ruin, destruction.
61 *away and clear* safe and free.

SCENE 4

Near Birnam Wood
Drum and colours. Enter Malcolm, Old Siward, Siward's Son, Macduff,
Menteith, Caithness, Angus, Lennox, Ross *and* Soldiers *marching.*

Malcolm
    Cousins, I hope the days are near at hand
    That chambers will be safe.
Menteith   We doubt it nothing.
Siward
    What wood is this before us?
Menteith   The wood of Birnam.
Malcolm
    Let every soldier hew him down a bough
    And bear't before him: thereby shall we shadow   5
    The numbers of our host, and make discovery
    Err in report of us.
Soldiers   It shall be done.
Siward
    We learn no other but the confident tyrant
    Keeps still in Dunsinane, and will endure
    Our setting down before't.
Malcolm   'Tis his main hope;   10
For where there is advantage to be gone,
Both more and less have given him the revolt,
And none serve with him but constrained things
Whose hearts are absent too.
Macduff   Let our just censures
    Attend the true event, and put we on   15
    Industrious soldiership.
Siward   The time approaches
    That will with due decision make us know
    What we shall say we have, and what we owe.
    Thoughts speculative their unsure hopes relate,
    But certain issue strokes must arbitrate;   20
    Towards which advance the war.

              They march off.

The Scottish army has now arrived near Birnam Wood and joined with the English army.

2 *That chambers . . . safe* when we can sleep safely in our beds. **What is Malcolm thinking of?**
2 *doubt it nothing* I don't have any doubt about it.
5–6 *shadow . . . host* disguise the size of our army.
6–7 *make discovery . . . us* cause those who are spying on us to give a false report.
8 *We learn no other but* all reports agree that.
9–10 *will endure . . . before 't* will allow us to lay seige to the castle.
10 Malcolm suggests that Macbeth's only hope is to 'stay put'. **Why should this be so?**
11–12 *For where . . . revolt* when there has been a favourable opportunity to desert him, soldiers of both high and low rank have taken it.
13 *constrained things* miserable creatures, forced to obey.
14–16 *Let our just . . . soldiership* let's save our opinion until after the event and, in the meantime, let's fight like good soldiers.
16–18 *The time . . . owe* the time will soon come when we can know with certainty what our real achievements are, rather than our mere expectations.
19–20 *Thoughts . . . arbitrate* talking only raises hopes; fighting brings results.

SCENE 5

Dunsinane. Inside Macbeth's castle.
Enter **Macbeth**, **Seyton** *and* **Soldiers**, *with drum and colours.*

Macbeth
    Hang out our banners on the outward walls;
    The cry is still, 'They come'. Our castle's strength
    Will laugh a siege to scorn: here let them lie
    Till famine and the ague eat them up.
    Were they not forc'd with those that should be ours,   5
    We might have met them dareful, beard to beard,
    And beat them backward home.

                 A cry of women within.

                      What is that noise?

Seyton
    It is the cry of women, my good lord.

               He leaves.

Macbeth
    I have almost forgot the taste of fears.
    The time has been my senses would have cool'd   10
    To hear a night-shriek, and my fell of hair
    Would at a dismal treatise rouse and stir
    As life were in't. I have supp'd full with horrors;
    Direness, familiar to my slaughterous thoughts,
    Cannot once start me.

               Re-enter Seyton

              Wherefore was that cry?   15

Seyton
    The Queen, my lord, is dead.

Macbeth
    She should have died hereafter;
    There would have been a time for such a word.
    Tomorrow, and to-morrow, and to-morrow,
    Creeps in this petty pace from day to day   20

Although still inside the walls of Macbeth's castle, the siege has taken place and the battle is about to begin.

1–3 In what mood do we find Macbeth?
3 *lie* stay.
4 *ague* fever.
5 *Were they . . . ours* if thy had not been reinforced with men who should have been fighting with me.
6 *met them . . . beard* gone out into the field defiantly to meet them face to face.
10 *my senses . . . cool'd* I would have felt the chill of fear.
11 *fell* scalp.
12 *dismal treatise* frightening tale.
13 *As* as if.
13 *I have supp'd . . . horrors* **What occasions might Macbeth have in mind?**
14–15 *Direness . . . me* horror has become so familiar to my violent way of thinking that it can never again startle me.
9–15 What is Macbeth suggesting about himself in these lines?
16 How do you think Lady Macbeth has died?
17 This could mean either that she would have died anyway at some time or other, or that had she died later and possibly in different circumstances, Macbeth could have given her death its proper recognition.
20–21 *Creeps . . . time* each day follows the next so painfully slowly until the end of time when the last syllable of history is finally written.

To the last syllable of recorded time,
And all our yesterdays have lighted fools
The way to dusty death. Out, out, brief candle!
Life's but a walking shadow, a poor player,
That struts and frets his hour upon the stage,   25
And then is heard no more; it is a tale
Told by an idiot, full of sound and fury,
Signifying nothing.

Enter a **Messenger**

Thou com'st to use thy tongue; thy story quickly.
Messenger
   Gracious my lord,   30
   I should report that which I say I saw,
   But know not how to do't.
Macbeth   Well, say, sir.
Messenger
   As I did stand my watch upon the hill,
   I look'd toward Birnam, and anon, methought
   The wood began to move.
Macbeth   Liar and slave!   35
Messenger
   Let me endure your wrath, if't be not so.
   Within this three mile may you see it coming;
   I say, a moving grove.
Macbeth   If thou speak'st false,
Upon the next tree shalt thou hang alive,
Till famine cling thee; if thy speech be sooth,   40
I care not if thou dost for me as much.
I pull in resolution, and begin
To doubt th'equivocation of the fiend
That lies like truth. 'Fear not, till Birnam wood
Do come to Dunsinane.' And now a wood   45
Comes toward Dunsinane. Arm, arm, and out!
If this which he avouches does appear,
There is nor flying hence nor tarrying here.
I gin to be aweary of the sun,
And wish th'estate o'th'world were now undone.   50
Ring the alarum bell! Blow wind! come wrack!

22–23 *All our . . . death* all the days that have gone by have served no other purpose than to provide a light for foolish men to find their way to death. **Why does Shakespeare describe death as *dusty*?**
23 *brief candle* **What does this refer to?**
24–27 What images does Shakespeare use in these lines to convey the pointlessness of life?
33 *As I . . . watch* while I was on duty.
34 *The wood began to move* **How will Macbeth react here?**
39 *next* nearest.
40 *Till . . . thee* until you shrivel up from starvation.
40 *sooth* the truth.
42–44 *I pull in . . . truth* I must check my confidence (like pulling in the reins of a horse) and question the double meanings of the fiend whose lies seem on the surface to be true.
46 *Arm, arm, and out* an order to attack.
47 *avouches* claims to be true.
48 *There is . . . here* I can't escape, nor can I stay here.
50 *th'estate . . . world* the established order in the world.
51 *wrack* wreck, destruction.

At least we'll die with harness on our back.

They leave

52 *harness* armour.

SCENE 6

Dunsinane. A plain before the castle.
Drum and colours. Enter Malcolm, Old Siward, Macduff *and their* Army
with boughs.

Malcolm
    Now, near enough; your leavy screens throw down,
    And show like those you are. You, worthy uncle,
    Shall with my cousin, your right noble son,
    Lead our first battle; worthy Macduff and we
    Shall take upon's what else remains to do,   5
    According to our order.
Siward   Fare you well.
    Do we but find the tyrant's power to-night,
    Let us be beaten, if we cannot fight.
Macduff
    Make all our trumpets speak; give them all breath,
    Those clamorous harbingers of blood and death.   10

They leave.

A parallel scene to the previous one, but from outside Macbeth's castle where the English and the Scottish armies prepare to attack.

1 *leavy* leafy. They are, of course, carrying the boughs from Birnam wood.
2 *show like those you are* show yourselves as you really are. **What else will become apparent to Macbeth when they remove the boughs?**
4 *we* the plural form used by members of the royal family.
6 *our order* our strategy. **What tone of voice does Malcolm assume here?**
7 *power* army.
7–8 *Do we but . . . cannot fight* if we can come face to face with Macbeth's army tonight, the only thing that would bring about defeat would be our own unworthy performance. In other words, Siward is encouraging everyone to do their best to overcome Macbeth, pointing out that the outcome is in their hands.
10 *clamorous harbingers* noisy messengers.

SCENE 7

Another part of the plain.
Enter Macbeth

Macbeth
    They have tied me to a stake; I cannot fly,

Macbeth is now outside the castle on the plain. **What does this suggest has happened?**

1 *tied me to a stake* In bear-baiting (a popular Elizabethan spectacle) the bear was tied to a stake and attacked by a pack of dogs until it was killed.

But bear-like I must fight the course. What's he
That was not born of woman? Such a one
Am I to fear, or none.

Enter Young Siward.

Young Siward
What is thy name?
Macbeth　　　　　Thou'lt be afraid to hear it.　　　　5
Young Siward
No; though thou call'st thyself a hotter name
Than any is in hell.
Macbeth　　　　　My name's Macbeth.
Young Siward
The devil himself could not pronounce a title
More hateful to mine ear.
Macbeth　　　　　　No, nor more fearful.
Young Siward
Thou liest, abhorred tyrant; with my sword　　　　10
I'll prove the lie thou speakst.

They fight and Young Siward *is slain.*

Macbeth　　　　　　Thou was born of woman:
But swords I smile at, weapons, laugh to scorn,
Brandish'd by man that's of a woman born.

He goes. Alarums. Enter Macduff.

Macduff
That way the noise is. Tyrant, show thy face.
If thou beest slain and with no stroke of mine,　　　15
My wife and children's ghosts will haunt me still.
I cannot strike at wretched kerns whose arms
Are hir'd to bear their staves: either thou, Macbeth,
Or else my sword with an unbattered edge
I sheathe again undeeded. There thou shouldst be;　　　20
By this great clatter, one of greatest note
Seems bruited. Let me find him, Fortune!
And more I beg not.

He goes. Alarums. Enter Malcolm *and* Old Siward.

2 *course* the round.
2–4 *What's he . . . none* Macbeth still clings on to the last prophecy despite the odds against him.
6 *a hotter name* **What does Young Siward suspect?**
10 *abhorred* hated.
11 *I'll prove the lie* prove it to be a lie.
16 *still* for ever.
17 *wretched kerns* the light armed footsoldiers that Macbeth has been forced to hire.
18 *staves* spears.
20 *undeeded* without having carried out any exploits in battle.
22 *bruited* proclaimed, reported.

Siward

    This way, my lord. The castle's gently rend'red;
    The tyrant's people on both sides do fight;   25
    The noble thanes do bravely in the war;
    The day almost itself professes yours,
    And little is to do.
Malcolm   We have met with foes
    That strike beside us.
Siward   Enter, sir, the castle.

                They enter. Alarum.

24 *gently render'd* surrendered with small resistance.
27 *The day . . . yours* you've almost won the day.
29 *strike beside us* joined our side in fighting. **What impression of the battle is given in lines 25 and 29?**

POINTS TO CONSIDER

Scene 2

? 13–14 *Some say . . . valiant fury* – we have not seen Macbeth since the beginning of Act 4. What is Shakespeare preparing us for?

? 20–22 *Now does . . . thief* – this image and the earlier one in lines 15–16 link with an earlier group of images. Which ones? What is suggested about Macbeth as king in these lines?

Scene 3

? 11–17 Macbeth hurls a succession of abuses at the Servant. What do these expressions suggest about Macbeth's state of mind?

? 32 *I'll fight . . . hack'd* what picture of Macbeth emerges here? What is the effect of *hack'd*? Where have we heard similar sentiments expressed?

? 50–51 *my land* indicates that the patient is no longer Lady Macbeth. Who is it? What links are there between the two in Macbeth's mind? How does the imagery re-inforce the link?

Scene 4

? 14–16 What note does Macduff introduce into the conversation?

Scene 5

? 1–3 What phrase in the previous scene has prepared us for Macbeth's mood?

? 9–15 What earlier quotations in the play provide a contrast to these sentiments?

? 42–44 Which *fiend* is Macbeth referring to? What truth has he only now begun to recognise?

? What aspects of Macbeth's character emerge in the last four lines of the scene?

Scene 6

? What function does this scene serve?

Scene 7

? 1 What does Macbeth suggest about himself in this image?

? *Young Siward is slain* – what purpose does his death serve?

? What is the effect on the audience of Macduff's exit in search of Macbeth?

ACT 5 SCENE 2–7 SUGGESTED ACTIVITIES

Production/Group Work

P1 In this part of the play the setting alternates between the inside and the outside of Macbeth's castle. Discuss in groups of four what simple means you could use as producer of the play to allow for a rapid change of scene. What effect does Shakespeare create with this rapid change?

P2 Although scene 4 is a very short scene, it does have several important dramatic functions. In groups of four, discuss the purpose of this scene. Pay particular attention to a) plot and b) the difference in character between Malcolm and Macduff.

P3 Macbeth's reaction to Lady Macbeth's death has been described as callous. In small groups, discuss the way he reacts to the news and, at the same time, consider all the changes that are taking place in his character and mood.

P4 How might the actor playing the part of Macbeth appear in scene 7? In small groups, discuss make-up, costume and any other effects that might be used to convey to the audience his present frame of mind?

Test

T1 a) Re-read Act 5 scene 5 lines 17–28. Then working in pairs but without the text, fill in the words missing from the speech below. (Write your words in a list on a separate sheet of paper, not in the book.) Try to use Shakespeare's original words if you can remember them. If not, use words that seem appropriate to you.

She should have died _____;
There would have been a _____ for such a word.
_____, and to-morrow, and to-morrow,
_____ in this _____ pace from day to day
To the last _____ of recorded time,
And all our _____ have lighted fools
The way to _____ death. Out, out, brief _____!
Life's but a walking _____, a poor _____,
That _____ and _____ his hour upon the stage,
And then is heard no more; it is a _____
Told by an _____, full of sound and _____,
Signifiying _____.

b) When you have finished, look at the speech in the text and write down the orignial words in a list next to your own. Now, with a partner, compare the two lists of words. If you have used different words, discuss with your partner what effect Shakepeare's words convey and how they are different from yours.

c) Still in pairs, and using Shakespeare's original words (from your second list), discuss what impression they give of Macbeth's view of life.

d) One person should read the speech aloud to the other. What impression does the *sound* of the speech give? Concentrate particularly on lines 19–21. How does Shakespeare manage to create this sound? Look at the punctuation.

T2 Add more images to your Image Trees.

Written

W1 Donalbain is mentioned in Act 5 scene 2 lines 7–8 but Shakespeare never tells us what happened to him. When did we last hear of Donalbain? Using your own imagination, write a paragraph describing what you think might have happened to him and explain why you think he did not join his brother in Scotland. When you have done this exercise, try to find out how Polanski made use of Donalbain at the end of his film of *Macbeth*.

W2 At the end of Act 5 scene 4 the Doctor vows never to return to Dunsinane again at any price. Imagine that he then goes home and records in his diary those details that he cannot, as a doctor, confide in anyone else. Write the entry for his diary for that day.

W3 Imagine that Lady Macbeth left a note before she died. What might she have written?

SCENE 8

Another part of the field.

Macbeth
> Why should I play the Roman fool, and die
> On mine own sword? Whiles I see lives, the gashes
> Do better upon them.

> *Enter* Macduff

Macduff   Turn, hell-hound, turn!

Macbeth
> Of all men else I have avoided thee.
> But get thee back, my soul is too much charg'd   5
> With blood of thine already.

Macduff   I have no words –
> My voice is in my sword: thou bloodier villain
> Than terms can give thee out!

> *They fight. Alarum.*

Macbeth   Thou losest labour.
> As easy mayst thou the intrenchant air
> With thy keen sword impress as make me bleed.   10
> Let fall thy blade on vulnerable crests;
> I bear a charmed life, which must not yield
> To one of woman born.

Macduff   Despair thy charm;
> And let the angel whom thou still hast serv'd
> Tell thee, Macduff was from his mother's womb   15
> Untimely ripp'd.

Macbeth
> Accursed be that tongue that tells me so,
> For it hath cow'd my better part of man:
> And be these juggling fiends no more believ'd
> That palter with us in a double sense;
> That keep the word of promise to our ear,
> And break it to our hope! I'll not fight with thee.

Macbeth appears with Macduff following closely behind.

1 *play the Roman fool* commit suicide. It was considered dishonourable for a Roman to be captured and many great men committed suicide rather than fall into enemy hands. **What is Macbeth's attitude to the Roman way?**

2–3 *Whiles I see . . . them* as long as there are enemies alive, it would be better to turn my sword upon them than myself.

3 *hell-hound* why does Macduff call Macbeth by this name?

4 *I have avoided thee* **Why?**

8 *Than terms . . . out* than words can describe.

They fight **Who will dominate?**

8 *Thou losest labour* you're wasting your energy.

9 *intrenchant* that cannot be cut.

10 *impress* mark, make an impression on.

11 *vulnerable crests* crests (on the helmets) of men who can be wounded. **What is Macbeth asking Macduff to do here?**

14 *angel* evil spirit.

16 *untimely ripp'd* prematurely removed by surgery, (that is, by a caesarian operation.) **Why does this line contain only two words? What will be the effect of these words on Macbeth and on the audience?**

18 *cow'd . . . man* subdued my spirit, crushed me.

19 *juggling fiends* **Why *juggling*?**

20 *palter* trick or trifle. *a double sense* using words ambiguously.

21–22 *That keep . . . hope!* they keep their promise in that in one sense the words turn out to be true; but in the other sense, on which our hope was based, the words prove to be false.

22 *I'll not fight with thee* **What are Macbeth's feelings at this moment?**

Macduff

> Then yield thee, coward,
> And live to be the show and gaze o'th'time.
> We'll have thee, as our rarer monsters are,   25
> Painted upon a pole, and underwrit,
> 'Here may you see the tyrant'.

Macbeth   I will not yield,

> To kiss the ground before young Malcolm's feet,
> And to be baited with the rabble's curse.
> Though Birnam wood be come to Dunsinane,   30
> And thou oppos'd, being of no woman born,
> Yet I will try the last. Before my body
> I throw my warlike shield: lay on, Macduff;
> And damn'd be him that first cries, 'Hold, enough!'

They go out, fighting. Alarums.

Retreat and flourish. Enter, with drums and colours, **Malcolm, Siward,**
> **Ross, Lennox, Angus, Caithness, Menteith** *and* **Soldiers.**

Malcolm

> I would the friends we miss were safe arriv'd.   35

Siward

> Some must go off; and yet, by these I see,
> So great a day as this is cheaply bought.

Malcolm

> Macduff is missing, and your noble son.

Ross

> Your son, my lord, has paid a soldier's debt:
> He only liv'd but till he was a man;   40
> The which no sooner had his prowess confirm'd
> In the unshrinking station where he fought,
> But like a man he died.

Siward   Then he is dead?

Ross

> Ay, and brought off the field. Your cause of sorrow
> Must not be measur'd by his worth, for then   45
> It hath no end.

Siward   Had he his hurts before?

24 *show . . . time* public spectacle of the age.

25 *rarer monsters* stranger freaks.

26 *Painted upon a pole* painted on a sign hanging on a pole. Macduff suggests that Macbeth should be exhibited as a freak at the circus. **Does this image give you a clear picture of what Macduff is saying?**

31 *oppos'd* standing in opposition to me.

31 *Yet . . . last* I'll fight to the death.

33 *Lay on* fight.

Retreat this would be the trumpet giving the official sound of defeat. *Flourish* in contrast would be Malcolm's trumpets sounding the note of triumph.

35 *I would . . . arriv'd* Malcolm refers to those who have not been accounted for.

36 *go off* die. *by these* judging by the number of men I can see.

38 *Macduff is missing* **What effect might this have on an audience who has just seen Macbeth and Macduff leave the stage fighting?**

39 *paid a soldier's debt* has been killed in action.

40 *He only . . . man* he only lived to early manhood.

41 *The which . . . confirm'd* no sooner had his courageous fighting proved him to be a man.

44–46 *Had he . . . before* was he wounded on the front of his body? **Why does Siward want to know this?**

Ross

    Ay, on the front.

Siward   Why, then, God's soldier be he!

    Had I as many sons as I have hairs,

    I would not wish them to a fairer death:

    And so his knell is knoll'd.

Malcolm   He's worth more sorrow,   50

    And that I'll spend for him.

Siward   He's worth no more;

    They say he parted well and paid his score:

    And so, God be with him! Here comes newer comfort.

              Re-enter **Macduff,** *with* **Macbeth's** head.

Macduff

    Hail, King! for so thou art. Behold where stands

    Th'usurper's cursed head: the time is free.   55

    I see thee compass'd with thy kingdom's pearl,

    That speak my salutation in their minds;

    Whose voices I desire aloud with mine –

    Hail, King of Scotland!

All   Hail, King of Scotland! (*Flourish*)

Malcolm

    We shall not spend a large expense of time   60

    Before we reckon with your several loves,

    And make us even with you. My Thanes and kinsmen,

    Henceforth be Earls, the first that ever Scotland

    In such an honour nam'd. What's more to do,

    Which would be planted newly with the time –   65

    As calling home our exil'd friends abroad

    That fled the snares of watchful tyranny;

    Producing forth the cruel ministers

    Of this dead butcher, and his fiend-like queen,

    Who, as 'tis thought, by self and violent hands   70

    Took off her life – this, and what needful else

    That calls upon us, by the grace of Grace,

    We will perform in measure, time, and place.

    So thanks to all at once and to each one,

    Whom we invite to see us crown'd at Scone.   75

               Flourish. They leave.

48 *hairs* a pun on heirs.

50 *his knell is knoll'd* the death-bell has been rung and there is no need to say more.

50 How does Malcolm react to Siward's calm acceptance of his son's death?

52 *parted* departed, died. *score* debts.

55 *The time is free* our age is now free from tyranny.

56 *Compass'd . . . pearl* surrounded by all that is good in your kingdom. Using the image of pearls, Macduff conveys the idea of the value of these Thanes to Malcolm and to the whole country.

57 *That speak . . . minds* who are greeting you in their hearts.

61–62 *Before . . . with you* before I repay you for your loyal services to me.

63 *Earls* an English title and so, in rewarding the Thanes in this way, Malcolm is also paying tribute to Edward and England.

64–65 *What's more . . . the time* whatever else must be done, ought to be done now, in this new era. **What image does Malcolm use here?**

67 *That fled . . . watchful tyranny* **Who might this refer to?**

68 *Producing forth* bringing to justice.

68 *ministers* agents. **When did Lady Macbeth associate herself with 'murd'ring ministers'?**

71 *Took off her life* confirmation here from Malcolm that Lady Macbeth did indeed commit suicide.

73 *We will . . . place* we'll carry all these things out in the proper order, time and place.

POINTS TO CONSIDER

? 4–6 What impression of Macbeth is given in these lines? What is your own attitude to him at this moment?

? 28 *young Malcolm* What earlier phrase does this echo?

? 29 *baited* taunted. Where has this image been used before?

? 34 Stage directions: *They go out fighting*. How much of the fight between Macbeth and Macduff should be shown? How would the Elizabethan audience react to the fighting? (See notes on 'An Afternoon at the Globe Theatre, p 4).

? 50 What is your reaction to Siward's calm acceptance of his son's death?

? *Re-enter Macduff with Macbeth's head*. What effect does Shakespeare create by showing Macbeth's death in this way?

? 69 *Of this dead . . . queen* Does this description sum up your own feelings towards Macbeth and Lady Macbeth?

? 60–75 What contrasts are implied here between Macbeth and Malcolm as rulers?

ACT FIVE SCENE 8 SUGGESTED ACTIVITIES

Production/Group Work

P1 Discuss in groups of four the way that Shakespeare handles the exchanges between Macbeth and Macduff in this scene. Consider the following points:
How much fighting between the two should be shown on stage?
How in producing the play would you stage the fighting?
Should Macbeth die on stage?
Would you have preferred Shakespeare to have dealt with Macbeth's death in a different way?

P2 In the same groups, discuss how you would interpret the following stage directions
Re-enter Macduff, with Macbeth's head.

P3 What qualities will Malcolm bring to the throne of Scotland? Do you think that he will be a good king? Discuss these questions in your groups.

Text

T1 In pairs, look again at lines 8–34. Prior to their final battle, Macbeth and Macduff have a war of words. Together try to pick out as many words as possible that contribute to this war. Look, in particular, for strong, challenging words. You should be able to find at least a dozen.

T2 Then, in the same pairs, take on a role each and read the lines aloud giving special emphasis the words you have picked out. What sounds do these words make?

T3 Add more images to your Image Trees. You should now have a number of completed Image Trees. These could be put together to represent Birnam Wood as a piece of class display work on *Macbeth*.

Written Work

W1 Many people react to Macbeth's death with mixed feelings. In a single paragraph, put into words what your own feelings are. Then try to explain why you feel like this.

Writing a Critical Review of *Macbeth*

1 Read the following critical review of a production of *Macbeth* at Stratford-upon-Avon written by Kenneth Tynan. The production (1955) starred Laurence Olivier as Macbeth and Vivien Leigh as Lady Macbeth.

Nobody has ever succeeded as Macbeth, and the reason is not far to seek. Instead of growing as the play proceeds, the hero shrinks; complex and many-levelled to begin with, he ends up a cornered thug, lacking even a death scene with which to regain lost stature. Most Macbeths, mindful of this, let off their big guns as soon as possible, and have usually shot their bolt by the time the dagger speech is out. The marvel of Sir Laurence Olivier's reading is that it reverses this procedure, turns the play inside out, and makes it (for the first time I can remember) a thing of mounting, not waning, excitement. Last Tuesday Sir Laurence shook hands with greatness, and within a week or so the performance will have ripened into a masterpiece: not of the superficial, booming, have-a-bash kind, but the real thing, a structure of perfect forethought and proportion, lit by flashes of intuitive lightning.

He begins in a perilously low key, the reason for which is soon revealed. This Macbeth is paralysed with guilt before the curtain rises, having already killed Duncan time and again in his mind. Far from recoiling and popping his eyes, he greets the air-drawn dagger with sad familiarity; it is a fixture in the crooked furniture of his brain. Uxoriousness leads him to the act, which unexpectedly purges him of remorse. Now the portrait swells; seeking security, he is seized with fits of desperate bewilder-ment as the prize is snatched out of reach. There was true agony in 'I had else been perfect'; Banquo's ghost was received with horrific torment, as if Macbeth should shriek 'I've been robbed', and the phrase about the dead rising to 'push us from our stools' was accompanied by a convulsive shoving gesture which few other actors would have risked....

The witches' cookery lesson is directed with amusing literalness; the Turk's nose, the Jew's liver and the baby's finger are all held up for separate scrutiny; but the apparitions are very unpersuasive, and one felt gooseflesh hardly at all. On the battlements Sir Laurence's throttled fury switches into top gear, and we see a lion, baffled but still colossal. 'I 'gin to be a-weary of the sun' held the very ecstasy of despair, the actor swaying with grief, his voice rising like hair on the crest of a trapped animal. 'Exeunt fighting' was a poor end for such a giant warrior. We wanted to see how he would die; and it was not he but Shakespeare who let us down.

Vivien Leigh's Lady Macbeth is more niminy-piminy than thundery-blundery, more viper than anaconda, but still quite competent in its small way. Macduff and his wife, actor-proof parts, are played with exceptional power by Keith Mitchell and Maxine Audley. The midnight hags, with traditional bonhomie, scream with laughter at their own jokes: I long, one day, to see whispering witches, less intent on yelling their sins across the country-side. The production has all the speed and clarity we associate with Glen Byam Shaw, and Roger Furse's settings are bleak and service-able, except for the England scene, which needs only a cat and a milestone to go straight into *Dick Whittington*.

2 Next, work in groups of four. The aim of the following exercise is to work out the role of a drama critic, basing some of your ideas on Kenneth Tynan's review. Forget about *Macbeth* for the moment and concentrate on the aspects of the play that are discussed. Take a large sheet of paper and write DRAMA CRITIC in the centre. Then draw at least ten stalks coming out of the centre. Try to fill each of these with those aspects of a play your group believes a drama critic should comment on.
DRAMA CRITIC

3 Now work alone. You have been asked to write a critical review of *Macbeth* for your school magazine or newspaper. Bearing in mind your group discussion on the role of the drama critic, write a review of the play. If you have seen a performance, you can use this as the basis of your article. If not, you may like to base your 'review' on some photos of more recent productions of *Macbeth* as well as your own study of the play and some of the class production exercises.

Past productions of *Macbeth*

Macbeth and Lady Macbeth

(Above left) The 1972 National Theatre production starred Anthony Hopkins and Diana Rigg, and used Elizabethan costume. Is this how you would expect Macbeth and Lady Macbeth to look?

(Above right) The American film Joe Macbeth *transferred the story to the Mafia underworld, with Macbeth as an Italian-American gang boss. Do you think that changing the time and place of the action like this can help people to understand the themes of the play?*

(Below left) The film Throne of Blood *portrayed Macbeth as a Japanese warlord. Would the play have to be altered much to be produced in this way? Would it help a Japanese audience to understand the themes of the play? Would it help a Western audience?*

The witches and the supernatural

(Above left) The BBC television production of Macbeth *was done in a studio, yet the 'blasted heath' where the witches meet seems very realistic. How else could you produce the setting for this scene?*

(Below left) Polanski's film version of Macbeth *gave the witches an interesting mixture of ages and costumes. Notice that the scene, which Shakespeare describes as taking place on a 'blasted heath', has been set on a beach. What difference would this make?*

(Above right) This is the line of Scottish kings descending from Banquo, which the witches show to Macbeth in Act Four, Scene 1. This stage production for the National Theatre in 1972 uses many actors and elaborate costumes for a very short scene in the play. Could the scene be done more simply? Do you think it would be easier to show Macbeth's visions on film or TV than on the stage?

What is *Macbeth* really about?

1 Read the following extract from James Thurber's *The Macbeth Murder Mystery* which shows one woman's very original interpretation of *Macbeth*.

'It was a stupid mistake to make,' said the American woman I had met at my hotel in the English lake country, 'but it was on the counter with the other Penguin books – the little sixpenny ones, you know, with the paper covers – and I supposed of course it was a detective story. All the others were detective stories. I'd read all the others, so I bought this one without really looking at it carefully. You can imagine how mad I was when I found it was Shakespeare.' I murmured something sympathetically. 'I don't see why the Penguin-books people had to get out Shakespeare plays in the same size and everything as the detective stories,' went on my companion. 'I think they have different-coloured jackets,' I said. 'Well I didn't notice that,' she said. 'Anyway, I got real comfy in bed that night and all ready to read a good mystery story and here I had *The Tragedy of Macbeth* a book for high-school students. Like *Ivanhoe*,' 'Or *Lorna Doone*, 'I said. 'Exactly,' said the American lady. 'And I was just crazy for a good Agatha Christie, or something. Hercule Poirot is my favourite detective.' 'Is he the rabbity one?' I asked. 'Oh, no,' said my crime-fiction expert. 'He's the Belgian one. You're thinking of Mr Pinkerton, the one that helps Inspector Bull. He's good, too.' Over her second cup of tea my companion began to tell the plot of a detective story that had fooled her completely – it seems it was the old family doctor all the time. But I cut in on her. 'Tell me,' I said. 'Did you read *Macbeth*?' 'I *had* to read it,' she said. 'There wasn't a scrap of anything else to read in the whole room.' 'Did you like it?' I asked. 'No, I did not,' she said decisively. 'In the first place, I don't think for a moment that Macbeth did it.' I looked at her blankly. 'Did what?' I asked. 'I don't think for a moment that he killed the King,' she said. 'I don't think the Macbeth woman was mixed up in it, either. You suspect them the most, of course, but those are the ones that are never guilty or shouldn't be, anyway.' 'I'm afraid,' I began, 'that I –' 'But don't you see?' said the American lady., 'It would spoil everything if you could figure out right away who did it. Shakespeare was too smart for that. I've read that people never have figured out *Hamlet*, so it isn't likely Shakespeare would have made *Macbeth* as simple as it seems.' I thought this over while I filled my pipe. 'Who do you suspect?' I asked, suddenly. 'Macduff,' she said, promptly. 'Good God,' I whispered softly.

'Oh Macduff did it, all right,' said the murder specialist. 'Hercule Poirot would have got him easily.' 'How did you figure it out?' I demanded. 'Well,' she said, 'I didn't right away. At first I suspected Banquo. And then, of course, he was the second person killed. That was good right in there, that part. The person you suspect of the first murder should always be the second victim.' 'Is that so?' I murmured. 'Oh, yes,' said my informant. 'They have to keep surprising you. Well, after the second murder I didn't know *who* the killer was for a while.' 'How about Malcolm and Donalbain, the King's sons?' I asked. 'As I remember it, they fled right after the first murder. That looks suspicious.' 'Too suspicious,' said the American lady. 'Much too suspicious. When they flee, they're never guilty. You can count on that.' 'I believe,' I said, 'I'll have a brandy,' and I summoned the waiter. My companion leaned toward me, her eyes bright, her teacup quivering. 'Do you know who discovered Duncan's body?' she demanded. I said I was sorry, but I had forgotten. 'Macduff discovers it,' she said, slipping into the historical present. 'Then he comes running downstairs and shouts. "Confusion has broke open the Lord's anointed temple" and "Sacrilegious murder has made his masterpiece" and on and on like that.' The good lady tapped me on the knee. 'All that stuff was rehearsed,' she said. 'You wouldn't say a lot of stuff like that, offhand, would you – if you had found a body?' She fixed me with a glittering eye. 'I –' I began. 'You're right!' she said. 'You wouldn't! Unless you'd practised it in advance. "My God, there's a body in here! is what an innocent man would say.' She sat back with a confident glare.

What seems to interest the American woman is *what happens* and *who did what*? In other words, her interest is in the STORY or the PLOT. While it is unlikely that Shakespeare intended the play to be seen as a detective story, the events that form the plot of *Macbeth* are obviously critically important.

In order to focus on the story and plot of *Macbeth* try one of the following exercises working alone.
Re-tell the *story* of *Macbeth*, either
● as a child's bedtime story,
● as a thriller, or
● as a sensational front page story in a Sunday newspaper.

2 At one level, Shakespeare was writing an exciting story which would entertain. But some things are surely missing when we look at *Macbeth* solely as a story. One of them is Shakespeare's language and the way he tells his story. This is his STYLE which we'll consider later (p 145). Shakespeare was also saying something about human nature and about the problems and issues that all of us have to face in life. *Macbeth* is an ancient Scottish nobleman, but he is also a man haunted by guilt and tormented by ambition. The ideas of guilt and ambition are two of the THEMES that run through the play. A theme is a recurring idea in a piece of writing and *Macbeth* contains many. Look again at the 'families' of images you have collected in your Image Trees. Each of these re-inforces an important theme in the play. Work out with your teacher what these themes are. Work out also what other themes run through the play. Then carry out the following exercise in groups to share the themes you have discovered.

3 Working in groups of about four, choose one theme. Write it down in the centre of a large sheet of paper. One person should act as *scribe* who writes down everything that comes out of your discussion which relates to this theme. It may be an event or a speech or simply your own response to what Shakespeare is saying about your theme. The diagram below may give you some suggestions for how to get started.

Art not without ambition, but without
The illness should attend it.
                                          Shalt be King hereafter

AMBITION

Macbeth and Lady Macbeth achieve their ambition but lose their peace of mind

4 When you have gathered as many ideas as possible, each group should *present* their theme to the other groups either
● as a mime,
● as role play, or
● as a modern version of the theme.

Friends and Foes – How we Judge People

Think about the difference between getting to know someone in real life and getting to know someone in a book. It's clearly going to be much easier in real life. We can talk to someone and establish a living relationship with them. It's something we do all the time and doesn't require a great deal of effort. It comes to us naturally and we soon tend to form a view about what we like or dislike about a person. Getting to know someone in literature is different. A great writer has the gift of creating character, but that character will only spring off the page if the reader wants it to, and that requires an effort of the imagination and our wholehearted involvement. Our response to a character in literature is a vital part of the creation of that character. Do the following exercises to make you think about getting to know and understand people.

1 Work in a group of four. Have a large sheet of paper and a felt tip pen. One person from the group should write, but all four should contribute ideas. In the centre of the sheet of paper, write the word CHARACTER in large letters. Then draw stems from all round the word and fill in all the different ways you can think of for finding out what a person's character is really like. You should be able to think of at least ten.

CHARACTER

2 Take another sheet of paper and, still working in the same group, choose one of the following characters from the play: Macbeth, Lady Macbeth, Banquo, Duncan, Malcolm, the Witches, Macduff. Write the name of the character you have chosen in large letters in the centre of your paper. Then, remembering the ideas you have already suggested for learning about character, fill in as many stems as possible with words describing the chosen character. To begin with, write down **every** suggestion that anyone in the group makes, even though you might not all agree. When you have finished, consider all the ideas on the paper and select ten that you can all agree upon. Finally, choose an incident from the play to illustrate each of your ideas.

3 You have been asked to prepare one of the following programmes on the character chosen for question 2.
- This is Your Life
- In the Psychiatrist's Chair
- Desert Island Discs

In your groups, choose your programme and prepare the material. Try to include as much information from the play as you can, but you may also use your imagination and add additional characters and events as needed. Prepare your script and then act out your programme for the other groups.

4 Your class is taking part in the radio programme *Just a Minute*. A team should be drawn up, with volunteers each prepared to talk for just a minute on a different character from the play, **without hesitation, repetition or deviation**. In other words, they must not pause, repeat themselves or move away from the subject. The other rules are as follows:
a The chairperson acts as timekeeper and his/her decision is final.
b Non-speakers may interrupt speakers and accuse them of hesitation, repetition or deviation.
c If the challenger is successful, then s/he wins a point. If not, the speaker wins a point.
d A successful challenger is then awarded the subject for the remainder of the minute (unless challenged by someone else).
e The points are awarded to the person speaking when the minute is up.
You will need a chairperson and someone to keep the score.

5 Now working alone choose one of the following titles and write about it. Use the text of the play as much as possible either to refer to incidents or to quote what people say.

- A Day in the Life of the Witches
- The Night I was invited to dinner with the Macbeths

In either case, do your best to make the characters come to life.

Shakespeare's Style

When we talk about STYLE, all we mean is the way in which a writer uses words in order to create an effect. Look at these two extracts from two different newspapers:

Phew! What a scorcher! London sizzles under steamy summer skies.

Today the London meteorological office confirmed that the average temperature this August had achieved new record levels.

These extracts are describing the same situation, but in very different ways. Notice, for example,

- the types of words used
- the kinds of pictures the writers conjure up

The differences that you have noticed come together under the heading of STYLE. Now look at these three extracts from *Macbeth*:

> *Out, out brief candle!*
> *Life's but a walking shadow, a poor player,*
> *That struts and frets his hour upon the stage,*
> *And then is heard no more.*

> *But in a sieve I'll thither sail,*
> *And like a rat without a tail,*
> *I'll do, I'll do, and I'll do.*

Knock, knock! Who's there? Faith, here's an English tailor come hither for stealing out of a French hose.

From these three extracts you can see how the same writer can produce very different effects by a change of style. Look at the picture of Shakespeare, the chef, on the right.

Shakespeare the Chef

A chef will vary his menu to cater for different tastes and for different occasions. Any changes are a result of a change of ingredients, that is, the different foods used in each recipe. Style, too, is made up of different 'ingredients' and these can be changed in just the same way. The following are the main 'ingredients' of a writer's style:

Presence or absence of rhyme and rhythm – VERSE OR PROSE
The pictures the writer introduces – IMAGERY
The words the writer chooses – DICTION
The mood or emotion the writer introduces – TONE

Let us now look closely at Shakespeare's style in 'Macbeth', taking these four 'ingredients' into particular consideration.

Verse and Prose in 'Macbeth'

When we study Shakespeare it is important to think about the way he uses verse and prose. Look at the following extracts and answer the questions below.

Here's a knocking indeed! If a man were porter of hell-gate, he should have old turning the key. Knock, knock, knock! Who's there, in th' name of Beelzebub?

> *Nought's had, all's spent,*
> *Where our desire is got without consent.*
> *'Tis safer to be that which we destroy,*
> *Than by destruction dwell in doubtful joy.*

1 Who is speaking the words in a) and b)?

2 What has just happened in each case to bring about these words?

3 Which is written in verse and which in prose?

These two extracts illustrate the use of verse and prose in Shakespeare's plays. Prose reflects the way we speak in our everyday lives. It doesn't rhyme, nor does it have a set rhythm. Shakespeare often reserved prose for comic or minor characters. Poetry, however, does have a particular rhythm and often rhymes. It was generally used for the main characters of the play because it was considered a better vehicle for intense emotion.

4 Find one example of prose and one example of poetry from 'Macbeth' that illustrate the points made above.

The flexibility of both prose and poetry is well illustrated in *Macbeth*. In the end Shakespeare made use of the form that best suited the emotions and the circumstances of the character at that moment in the play, irrespective of whether it was a major or a minor character.

5 Find an example of prose used by a major character in 'Macbeth'.

6 Why does prose seem appropriate in your example?

Shakespeare's Verse

Methought I heàrd a voìce cry "Slèep no mòre;
Macbèth does mùrder slèep" – the ìnnocent slèep....

7 Read these two lines aloud and notice the oblique line (like this `) above each word you stress. Each line has been marked in five places on the stress. Now mark these two lines in the same way with an oblique line.

Good things of day begin to droop and drowse,
Whiles night's black agents to their preys do rouse

You will notice that these lines rhyme. Much of the verse Shakespeare uses in his plays does not rhyme and is known as BLANK VERSE. You will also see that each line consists of five weak syllables each followed by five strong syllables. (The strong ones are the ones you have marked.) This rhythm of five weak and five strong syllables is known as IAMBIC PENTAMETER. Shakespeare made full use of the iambic pentameter in all his plays.

One of the reasons that the iambic pentameter was so appealing was its similarity to the rhythm of spoken English.

8 Read the following two lines of dialogue aloud.

'Get up you lazy child and make your bed'.
'I will as soon as I can find my clothes.'

Iambic Pentameter

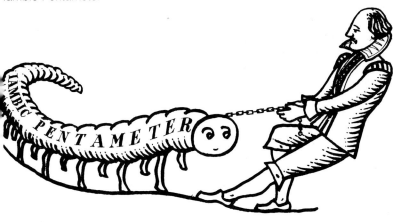

As in the previous exercise, mark with an oblique each word you stress as you say it aloud. Again you should have marked five words.

Not all our speech sounds exactly like this, but much of what we say does fall into the pattern of one weak syllable followed by one strong. From this example, it is possible to see how the rhythm Shakespeare chose in his writing allowed his characters to sound as though they were speaking quite naturally, even though they were often using verse.

9 Look at Lady Macbeth's speech in Act 1, scene 7 lines 60–73. Read this speech aloud carefully and deliberately stressing the five beats in each line. (Did you find any lines with more or less than five strong beats? There are variations and irregularities in nearly all the speeches.) Now read it again, this time as though it is written in continuous prose form (as in a novel). What is the difference in sound between your two readings? What makes it so easy to read the speech the second way, that is, as though it is prose, not poetry? Which one would you choose if you were acting this part in the play and why?

Although most of 'Macbeth' is written either in prose or in blank verse using the iambic pentameter, there are some notable exceptions to this. The most significant of these is found in the Witches' scenes.

10 Look at the following lines:

Fillet of a fenny snake,
In the cauldron boil and bake;
Eye of newt, and toe of frog,
Wool of bat, and tongue of dog,
Adder's fork, and blind-worm's sting,
Lizard's leg, and howlet's wing

How many beats are there to a line? Mark each one with an oblique line.

11 Listen to the sound of this rhythm. Which consonants are repeated? Do the sounds of the words and the beat of the rhythm remind you of anything?

12 Why do you think Shakespeare chose to introduce a completely different rhythm for each of the Witches' scenes?

Imagery in 'Macbeth'

We have already described imagery, another of the 'ingredients' of style, as referring to the pictures that a writer conjures up in his work. We all use imagery in our everyday conversation. Rather than saying 'It's raining heavily', we might say 'It's raining cats and dogs'. Instead of saying 'You've given away the secret', we might say, 'You've let the cat out of the bag'. These statements are obviously not literally true, but through the pictures they conjure up, they make our point more vividly and forcefully than a literal statement.

Writers use imagery for the same reason we all do – to make a point more strongly. Take, for example, this image from 'Macbeth'.

look like the innocent flower,
But be the serpent under't.

Lady Macbeth is here encouraging Macbeth to enter the world of deception with her and to hide his evil thoughts behind an innocent expression. Imagine what this would look like as a picture.

Innocent flower

The picture of the flower with the serpent lurking underneath it makes this idea a far clearer one. The serpent is associated with evil. But the image also introduces into the play the idea that appearances will be deceptive, people may not always be what they seem. This image, therefore, has served a double purpose. It makes a point more clearly. It also introduces an important theme.

Look at another example:

> *Sleep that knits up the ravell'd sleave of care,*
> *The death of each day's life, sore labour's bath,*
> *Balm of hurt minds, great nature's second course,*
> *Chief nourisher in life's feast.*

1 Pick out *five* different images referring to sleep.

2 What do these images together suggest about sleep?

3 Where else in the play is sleep looked at in this way?

From these examples you can see that Shakespeare uses everyday images which would be familiar to most of his audience. By picking upon common ideas such as sleep, nature and animals, he was able to play upon the imagination of both the educated and uneducated members of his audience.

Macbeth's first words on hearing the truth of the Witches' prophecy are

> *The Thane of Cawdor lives; why do you dress me*
> *In borrowed robes? Three.3.109–111*

4 What image here does Macbeth use to describe the new title offered to him?

5 Is it an appropriate image? Does it make the idea easier to understand?

6 Find three more examples of images of clothes from 'Macbeth'.

7 Find two images from each of the following groups. In each case try to decide what picture the image brings to mind and whether Shakespeare has been successful in playing upon your imagination.
DISEASE; FOOD; SLEEP; ANIMALS; NATURE (gardening, planting, roots); DAY AND NIGHT (light and darkness); WATER.

8 What idea is suggested by each of your images? Does this idea appear anywhere else in the play?

Diction in 'Macbeth'
Look at this passage spoken by Lady Macbeth:

> *Come you spirits*
> *That tend on mortal thoughts, unsex me here;*
> *And fill me, from the crown to the toe, topfull*
> *Of direst cruelty. Make thick my blood,*
> *Stop up the access and passage to remorse,*
> *That no compunctious visitings of nature*

Shake my fell purpose nor keep peace between
The effect and it.   One.5.lines 40–47

1 What impression of Lady Macbeth's character emerges from this passage?

2 Read this passage aloud. Certain consonant sounds are repeated over and over again. Which sounds are these? Write down words containing these sounds. Are they pleasant or unpleasant sounds? Do they remind you of anything else?

3 Look at the rest of Lady Macbeth's speech. Can you now add other words to your list that have the same effect?

Next look at the following speeches from Duncan and Banquo

Duncan
This castle hath a pleasant seat; the air
Nimbly and sweetly recommends itself
Unto our gentle senses.
Banquo   *This guest of summer*
The templehaunting martlet, does approve
By his lov'd mansionry that the heaven's breath
Smells wooingly here;

4 What atmosphere is Shakespeare creating here?

5 Read the extract aloud. You will notice that the letter 's' is also very important in this piece but this time it sounds different from the 's' sound in the speech describing Lady Macbeth. How and why? Pick out another soft-sounding consonant that is repeatedly used above.

6 From each line pick out one or two words that have attractive or appealing associations and notice how many of them contain some of the sounds you have already listed.

From these exercises, it should now be clear that Shakespeare chooses his words carefully, so that the meaning and the sound reinforce each other. Look at the following speeches and answer the same questions on them as you have on the two extracts above.

Malcolm's speech (Four.3.lines 57–65)
Third Witch (Four.1.lines 22–32)
Macbeth's speech (One.7.lines 1–7)

Tone in 'Macbeth'

Another important area to think about in style is TONE. Consider for a moment, the way we use our own voices when we talk to each other. We convey our emotions to a large extent by the tone of voice we use. Anger, joy, irritation, sorrow, bewilderment, amusement and so on can all be communicated through tone. For example, the phrase 'I'll do it' can convey a very wide range of emotions simply through the tone of voice. 'I'll do it' carries a very different message from 'I'll *do* it.

1 Say a simple phrase like, 'I won't tell him'. aloud in as many ways as possible. How many different emotions can you convey?

2 Find speeches in 'Macbeth' that convey the following emotions:
FEAR, GREED, ANGER, SORROW, IMPATIENCE, CONTENTMENT, CONFIDENCE.

3 Can you find an example of any other emotion in the play? There is a clue in the picture below.

LIAR AND SLAVE!

Sometimes we use TONE in a more complicated, subtle way. For example, in order to give words greater impact, someone might say the opposite of what they mean. To the pupil who has a frivolous answer to every question, the teacher may snap, 'We are being clever today aren't we?' The message that is conveyed is totally different from the words that are actually spoken. This is, in fact, an example of IRONY. 'What a beautiful day it is!' someone might say, when it is in fact, pouring with rain. The use of irony here simply serves to emphasise the atrocious weather. Irony allows us to express an emotion indirectly and therefore, if handled delicately, with greater subtlety.

A form of irony that Shakespeare often uses in 'Macbeth' is DRAMATIC IRONY. This is the sort of irony that occurs when a character is not entirely aware of the real or full significance of his words. Usually the audience is fully aware of the irony because they know something that the character does not. When Duncan turns to the newly made Thane of Cawdor and addresses him as 'My worthy Cawdor!'(I.iv.47) the audience is fully aware that Macbeth is already plotting against the life of the king. Duncan's words, therefore, are an example of dramatic irony since the audience realizes that Macbeth is far from worthy. 'Macbeth' is full of examples of dramatic irony because it is a play in which the characters, Macbeth and Lady Macbeth in particular, only gradually learn the real significance of their words, thoughts and actions.

4 Look at the rest of Duncan's words in scene iv of Act I. Can you find any other examples of dramatic irony?
5 By using dramatic irony, what does Shakespeare suggest to us about the character of Duncan?
6 What emotions are created in the audience by the use of dramatic irony in this scene?
7 There are many other examples of dramatic irony in 'Macbeth'. Find three separate scenes in which there is dramatic irony at the expense of
● Macbeth
● Lady Macbeth
● Banquo.

Tragedy—People and Events

Today the word *tragedy* is widely and commonly used. Newspapers and TV reports often describe an accident or disaster as a 'tragedy'. A plane crash, a ferry sinking, a fire in a football stand or a terrorist hi-jack have all been described in this way. Sometimes also, the media will describe the unexpected serious illness of an individual as a 'tragedy' or 'tragic'. These events are usually seen as tragic because of the number of people killed or because they are totally unexpected and accidental. One of our central modern ideas about tragedy concerns the waste involved and the often unnecessary nature of disastrous events.

These are common and widely accepted views of tragedy today, but not ones that Shakespeare would have understood. For Shakespeare, tragedy was not an accident or a disastrous event on a large scale, or the onset of illness; it was something that happened to an individual. In his eyes, tragedy occurred when a man or woman, through an error of judgement or some weakness in their character, suffered major misfortune and even death. The tragedy became all the greater when the individual was of high rank for the impact of that person's decline might well affect family, friends, even a whole nation.

Shakespeare's view of tragedy is one that was held by ancient writers such as Aristotle. Aristotle was an early Greek writer who believed that a tragedy took place when a person of high rank and responsibility suffered downfall and misfortune, not through depravity or vice, but by some error of judgement or weakness. This view of tragedy helps to explain why Shakespeare wrote his tragedies in the way he did. Look at the diagram below. In order to understand in what ways Shakespeare's view of tragedy is different from our own, fill in the space under MODERN VIEW. Each point you make will probably provide a contrast to the point made under SHAKESPEARE'S VIEW. Number one has been done for you.

WHAT IS TRAGEDY?

SHAKESPEARE'S VIEW	MODERN VIEW
1 involves an individual	**1** often involves many people
2 that person is of high rank	**2**
3 caused by error of judgement or human weakness	**3**
4 events lead to individual suffering and eventual death	**4**

SENSE OF WASTE
LOSS OF LIFE
UNFULFILLED POTENTIAL
INDIVIDUAL SUFFERING
GENERAL SUFFERING
FEELING OF 'IF ONLY'

The following activities should enable you to explore together in what ways *Macbeth* is a tragedy in Shakespeare's terms as well as our own.

Activities

1 In groups of four, discuss the following:
a) In what ways do you consider Macbeth to be a man with the qualities of a hero?
b) What is Macbeth's major weakness?
c) Do you think that Macbeth suffered from an error of judgement?
d) What might have happened to Macbeth if he had not killed Duncan?

e) Consider what would have happened to Macbeth
  • without his wife.
  • without the Witches.
2 Still in groups, discuss how the tragedy of Macbeth affects
a) his family
b) his friends
c) the whole nation.

3 In pairs, draw a diagram to show how Macbeth is subject to good an⸝
evil influences throughout the play. A suggestion for how you might d⸝
this is given below. When you have drawn your diagram, mark th⸝
stages at which the tragedy might have been averted.

4 On your own, write a list of reasons why Macbeth might be describe⸝
as a 'tragic hero'.

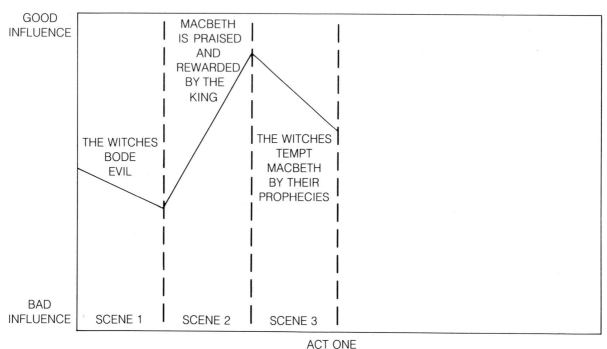

Glossary

Anaconda a gigantic South American water-boa (snake)

Blank verse verse which does not rhyme, usually iambic pentameter

Diction the choice of words a writer makes to create a particular effect or tone

Divine right of kings the belief that a king was God's representative on earth: a crime against a king was therefore also an offence against God

Dumb show the story of a play performed in actions but without words

Equivocation telling a misleading half-truth

Euphemism using a pleasant form of words to describe something unpleasant or distasteful.

Familiar an assistant to a witch, usually in the form of an animal

Gallery the tiered seats around the walls of the Elizabethan theatre

Gatherer the money collecter in the Elizabethan theatre

Groundlings the poorer people who paid one penny to stand in the pit of the theatre

iambic pentameter a rhythm form which consists of unstressed (˘) and stressed (`) syllables in patterns of five as in:
    Ŏ fŭll ŏf scòrpiŏns ĭs̀ m̀y mind, dĕar ẁife!

imagery the use of language to appeal to the senses, word pictures. Imagery normally involves the comparison of two unrelated objects or ideas

irony saying the opposite of what is meant. It involves two layers of meaning: a surface meaning and the real meaning beneath the surface

Patron typically a wealthy supporter of writers and artists. In return for this assistance (called patronage), poems and plays were often dedicated to the partron.

Personification describing inanimate or non-living objects in terms of people or animals, giving them minds or feelings

Pit the standing area in the Elizabethan theatre

Props short for property, that is, any article required on stage

Prose the ordinary form of spoken or written language without an obvious rhythm

Pun a play upon words alike in sound but different in meaning

Sack an old name for Spanish wine

Soliloquy a speech delivered by a character direct to the audience, which is usually used to convey the character's innermost thoughts. Other characters may be present, but they do not 'hear' what is said. It is a private communication between the speaker and the audience.

Spectacle the sight of a show or a pageant

Stressed syllable the syllable in a line of poetry on which the emphasis falls when the line is read aloud or spoken

Style the way in which a writer uses words that is distinctive to that particular writer

Theme the central idea in a piece of writing

Tiring house the area behind the stage where actors dressed or 'attired'.

Tone the attitude taken by the writer to the subject matter; the prevailing feeling behind the writing

Uxoriousness excessive fondness for a wife.

Verse the rhyme and rhythm that creates the form and shape of poetry

Wherry a shallow, light boat